Strong Leadership

Strong Influence

Harnessing the Effective Mindsets, Principles, and Strategies of the World's Highly Successful Leaders

Tim Wealth

<u>Disclaimer</u>

Contents

Acknowledgement

In the journey of writing "Strong Leadership, Strong Influence: Harnessing the Effective Mindsets, Principles, and Strategies of the World's Highly Successful Leaders," I was fortunate to be surrounded by an extraordinary group of people whose support and ideas were helpful.

First and foremost, I want to thank my family. Their unfailing encouragement, patience, and faith in my vision have been the foundation of my endeavor. Thank you to my spouse for the numerous cups of coffee and late-night chats that shaped many of the concepts in this book.

I am grateful to my mentor, Dr. Jane Smart, whose wisdom and counsel not only inspired my professional trajectory but also served as a foundation for the creation of this book. Her leadership insights have helped shape my thinking and attitudes.

A particular thank you to my business colleagues and peers, whose experiences and tales have greatly enriched this book. Your shared leadership struggles and achievements have been crucial in adding authenticity and depth to this work.

To the Bright Horizon Publishing team, particularly Sarah Johnson, my editor, whose sharp eye and intelligent comments have substantially improved the quality of this text. Your professionalism and commitment have been outstanding.

My greatest gratitude goes to the many executives from a variety of industries who volunteered to be interviewed for this book. Your willingness to share your experiences, trials, and triumphs has brought vital real-world insights into the art of leadership.

I would also want to thank the academic and professional communities for their resources and research, which were critical in supporting the concepts and tactics described in this book.

Finally, thank you for taking the time to read this. This book was written to motivate and encourage present and potential leaders, and your participation in these concepts helps to achieve this aim.

Thank you,

Tim Wealth

What People Who Used This Book Are Saying

"Tim Wealth's book is a game changer for leaders." His insights on effective attitudes and techniques have had a significant impact on my leadership style." *Sophia Zhang, Zenith Innovations CEO*

"Wealth's book is a goldmine for any leader." It's unusual to find such a blend of depth and realism in leadership books." - *David Kim, Founder and CEO, FutureTech Ventures*

"As a business leader, I found Wealth's book to be instructive. His thoughts on influence and decision-making are game changers in the field of leadership." *Emily Johnson, Chief Financial Officer of Global Finance Inc.*

"Tim Wealth brings a new and impactful approach to leadership." His work is essential reading for anybody seeking to lead in today's challenging corporate world." *Michael Smith, Apex Consulting Group Senior Partner*

"In all my years of business, I have never come across a more comprehensive guide to leadership." Wealth's combination of theory and practice is unrivaled." - ***Rajiv Patel, Quantum Corp.'s Director, International Business Development***

"The book by Wealth is a masterclass in effective leadership." His practical guidance and ideas are priceless for anybody trying to increase their impact." - ***Linda Garcia, Vice President of Marketing, Creative Solutions Inc.***

"A transformative handbook for today's leaders." Tim Wealth's book is full of knowledge and concrete methods that have changed the way I lead." - ***Amir Khan, Founder, TechVenture Solutions***

"This book is essential for understanding successful leadership principles." Tim Wealth has done an outstanding job in offering a complete leadership handbook." - ***Emma Thompson, Chief Strategy Officer, Dynamic Enterprises'***

"Wealth's book is not only informative but also truly inspiring." It's a must-have for everyone who wants to learn the art of leading." - Carlos Alvarez, ***Director, Global Strategies Group Managing***

Strong Leadership Strong Influence

"Tim Wealth's leadership insights are both profound and practical." His work is an invaluable resource for all levels of leadership." - *Natasha Ivanova, Head of Operations, East European Logistics*

Introduction

You Too Can Be Highly Successful

"Success is not how high you have climbed, but how you make a positive difference to the world." – Roy T. Bennett

Every individual defines success differently. Everyone strives for success, whether it is in their career, their home, or their family. When you achieve your goals, you feel proud, it pushes you to do better, and it lets you know you've made an effect in a competitive environment.

Every man desire success. He desires a pleasant life. At the very least, he has enough money to support himself without going into debt. They are capable of progressing in life. Aspiring to be the next Jeff Bezos, Bill Gates, or Mark Zuckerberg is no longer necessary. Still, if you try to emulate the leadership style of strong leaders by learning their secrets, you will be among the world's most successful leaders.

Following the success route is difficult, but it is not impossible. In this book, I have established certain principles you can follow to become one of the "World's successful leaders" of the future.

The first step is to invest in yourself. Investing in oneself entails reading a book, learning new sciences, and absorbing knowledge. There was a time when studying new sciences required hard labor and great distance travel, but in the age of social media, learning new sciences is no longer such a difficult undertaking. This is simple to perform at home using the Internet.

YouTube may be used to learn new things, online tutors can be found, and online books can be read.

Another crucial aspect of success is never to compare yourself to others. Learn to be satisfied with what God has provided for you.

Man can never get beyond a certain point. Every human being possesses a capacity. Some have less than others, but there must be a limit. A single person can only go so far, but you can accomplish much more with a solid team. Every successful person in the world achieved their achievement as part of a team. Steve Jobs was an excellent team player and leader. Mark Zuckerberg is also a big fan of his team. So, surround yourself with decent and worthwhile individuals. Gather people who believe positively and are honest, truthful, kind, and honest.

Never be a prisoner of your past; move on while accepting your history. Remember that life is about progress; don't ruin your future by dwelling on the past. The past is just there to help you 'move through' and learn from your mistakes. When a person becomes stuck in the past, his present also becomes stuck. He is unable to proceed. He has no control over himself, and his history eventually affects his present.

What happened has ended. Just get on with it. You cannot change the past or go back in time. So, learn from the past and begin living in the present for your future to be better than your past.

Self-respect is another guiding principle. Begin appreciating yourself right now. The way you treat yourself determines the way others will treat you. Before going to bed, hold yourself accountable. Assess yourself objectively.

Finally, the most important thing to remember is that your future is heavily influenced by how you think today. Always think positively and constructively. A man receives what he believes. The "Law of Attraction" is a natural law that we draw upon. According to this, if a person thinks favorably, the universe's positive energy surrounds him, and if a person thinks badly, the universe's negative energy surrounds him. This power has a significant impact on a person's personality.

A man should not be subjected to his thoughts; his thoughts should be subjected to him. It is difficult work, but you can solve numerous difficulties once you manage your mind. The road to success will become less difficult.

This Book Purpose

This book does not teach you how to be successful by chance or luck. Success does not happen by accident or chance; it is the result of adhering to certain principles. Success is a highly personal concept. How can one tell if someone is successful? Personal fortune and power? The ability to bring about change? Personal fulfillment and happiness?

Success may be the most enigmatic of our regularly used words, yet a few people seem to embody it so completely that it's impossible to dispute that they are some of the world's most successful leaders.

This book will make you aware of new possibilities. It digs into the profound thoughts and methods that have contributed to the success of some of the world's most successful leaders. This book tries to unearth the hidden secrets contributing to these high achievers' outstanding impact on the world by comprehensively analyzing their mindsets, philosophies, and techniques.

The voyage begins with a dissection of successful leaders' mindsets, showing the cognitive patterns that distinguish them. Furthermore, the book delves into the guiding ideas that have been the cornerstones of these people's success. These values serve as lighthouses for people seeking to leave a lasting impression, whether through inventive thinking, tenacity in the face of adversity, or a commitment to continual learning.

The book then delves into the precise tactics successful leaders use in various fields, providing readers with practical ideas they may use in their lives. Each method, from effective time management to strategic decision-making, is portrayed as a helpful tool for personal and professional development.

By revealing the secrets of the world's most successful leaders, I hope not only to inspire but also to guide readers in cultivating their success. In this book, I lay a road map for anyone who wants to comprehend and live the attitude, concepts, and methods that lead to amazing success.

Prepare for a life-changing trip as you unearth the hidden truths that have impacted the lives of the world's most successful leaders. **"Strong Success Strong Influence"** shines with knowledge, directing readers toward success, influence, and long-term effective impact

Chapter 1

Cultivating Success Mindsets

"A successful mindset isn't about winning every time, but learning and growing from every experience. True success comes from understanding that failure is a stepping stone, not a stopping point." – John C. Maxwell

T alents and skills are valuable assets because they pave the road for those who possess them. Talent and skill, however, do not ensure success because some people are extraordinarily talented and have the finest abilities yet fail. As a result, being skilled or brilliant in your chosen profession does not guarantee success and happiness in life.

In other words, your expertise needs something to surge and set you apart from your peers. God freely gave you talent and skill, but you can't purchase the proper attitude; it's priceless and the result of the right mindset. The correct mentality is a virtue that you cultivate rather than a gift. Cultivation involves seed sowing and growth. It suggests that the appropriate attitude is like a seed you nurture until it matures. Combined with your ability or expertise, it will propel you far beyond your peers.

In the quest for excellence, your mentality serves as the compass that guides your path. As a person motivated by ambition and a constant desire for a life well-lived, you recognize that success is defined not only by the destination but also by the attitude with which you begin the trip. Welcome to the realm of the success mentality – a mindset that enables you to approach any activity with a winning attitude and open the door to amazing accomplishments.

The Success Mindset's Essence

Consider your attitude to be the lens through which you see the world. The success attitude acts as a magnifying glass, fueling your drive and propelling you to continually seek the best. It is the conviction that excellence results from purposeful choices and a commitment to ongoing progress.

The excellence attitude is your guiding star in a world where success is frequently the result of constant work and devotion. No matter where you are in your career, developing this mentality places you as a leader in your sector and a catalyst for your objectives.

The Influence of Positive Attitude

A positive attitude — the notion that problems are opportunities, failures are transient, and achievement is within your reach — is at the heart of the excellent mentality. A good attitude impacts your decisions, forms your behaviors, and decides your consequences.

2

A positive attitude lets you approach life's obstacles with a solution-focused perspective. It's the force that allows you to convert barriers into stepping stones, see possibilities in adversity, and stay focused on the broader picture.

The Achievement Journey

Cultivating a success attitude requires self-awareness, resilience, and a commitment to improvement. Here are three concrete measures to take to begin this revolutionary journey:

1.   Establish High Expectations

Set a higher standard for yourself. Rather than settling for mediocrity, aim for greatness in all you do. Set high expectations for the quality of your work, the breadth of your knowledge, and the significance of your contributions.

2.   Accept Continuous Improvement

Consider every situation an opportunity to learn and grow. Seek feedback, discover areas for improvement, and continually push yourself to outperform your prior successes.

3.   Develop a Solution-Oriented Mindset

Focus on solutions rather than issues when confronted with difficulties. Train your mind to look for possibilities in challenges and to attack hurdles with an innovative mentality.

Activate Your Success Potential

As a seasoned life coach, I've seen the transformational power of the success attitude in people's lives. By adopting this attitude, you are living a concept of constant progress and persistent devotion rather than merely seeking achievement.

Every action becomes a chance for greatness. Your ability to approach every activity with an outstanding attitude distinguishes you as a light of inspiration, whether engaging with clients, managing teams, or achieving personal ambitions.

So, are you ready to embrace an excellent mindset? Are you willing to see obstacles as stepping stones and approach every opportunity optimistically? The decision is yours, and the adventure begins right now.

Enter the land of the excellence mentality, where every activity leads to spectacular results.

Pattern of Thought in Successful People

Successful individuals have a unique perspective on the world. They are not flawless. And they don't have it any easier than you do.

But they constantly appear to be on the go.

Regardless of the hurdles they face. Regardless of the obstacles in their path. Regardless of how loudly doubters doubt or detractors scoff.

They find a way to triumph.

How? They believe in a few crucial elements that will make or break their quest for success. According to them, these views aren't merely motivational statements they read once in a book.

What successful individuals think affects every aspect of their everyday lives. Here are 10 mental thinking patterns of extremely successful individuals that you might implement in your own life.

1.   They Think "Specificity"

Successful people grasp the art of goal-setting by being as explicit as possible. Instead of making general statements like "I want to get more sleep" or "I need to lose weight," they will make objectives like "I'm going to be in bed by 9:30 on weeknights starting tonight" or "I'm going to lose 10 pounds by eating salads for lunch and walking after dinner."

They use that specificity in business by saying things like, "I'm going to get five new clients this week by calling five prospects every day."

Defining the objective makes identifying the actionable steps needed to make it a reality easier. You are more driven to follow through when you know exactly what you want to do.

2.   They Think "Time consciousness"

A day consists of 1,440 minutes. Successful people understand this and squander a few minutes each day as much as possible. They recognize that they will never be able to regain even a single minute spent on pointless chores and activities.

Mark Zuckerberg circumvented this by wearing the same clothing almost every day for years. He was mocked, but Zuck's distinctive grey t-shirt saved him a lot of time in the morning. Instead of wasting time browsing through his closet, his selection was easy, allowing him to focus on more essential matters.

Elon Musk follows a strict schedule by dividing his calendar into five-minute increments.

3.   They Think "Teamwork"

They understand that it is the team that triumphs. Michael Jordan is, without a doubt, one of the best basketball players of all time, but playing with legends like Scottie Pippen, Horace Grant, and Dennis Rodman during his career helped mold Jordan into the superstar he is today. "The strength of the team is each member," declared his former coach, Phil Jackson. The team's strength is the strength of each member."

Successful individuals look for people with whom they can cooperate, as well as those who complement their own talents and flaws. I've worked hard to surround myself with the greatest staff possible. This stimulates and drives me to improve tenfold. The "I can do it myself" thought habit prevents most individuals from achieving success. Get rid of it and begin to think, "I can only do it with others."

4.   They Think "Continuous Learning"

Successful individuals make time to read, attend seminars, attend workshops, and watch informative webinars. They understand the importance of honing existing talents and learning new ones. So can you if Bill Gates, Warren Buffett, and Oprah Winfrey fit reading into their schedules. Before bed, read a book or listen to a podcast on your commute. You may listen to a book or podcast while exercising or attend an online class over your lunch break.

"It is one of the primary ways that I learn and has been since I was a child," Gates says of reading. I also get to visit intriguing sites, interact with scientists, and hear a lot of courses online these days. But reading is still my primary method of learning new topics and testing my comprehension."

5. **They Think "Emotional Intelligence Development."**
Emotional intelligence is the capacity to recognize your own emotions and those of others around you. It aids in problem-solving and motivating others. Even if you were not born with high emotional intelligence, successful people search for methods to improve it by:

• Not being a perfectionist.

• Understanding how to strike a balance between work and recreation.

• Being open to new experiences.

• Getting rid of distractions.

• Demonstrating empathy.

• Recognizing your talents and shortcomings.

• Having self-motivation.

• Concentrating on the good.

• Establishing limits.

6. **They Think "Positivism"**
Positive thinking is essential for setting tough objectives, but successful individuals never underestimate the difficulty of achieving such goals. According to research, realistic optimists are happier and have more control over themselves and their emotions than unrealistic optimists.

"When faced with a task, obstacle, or issue, they never declare, 'This is the only thing I can do, and I have no other options.' They'll be inventive, having A, B, and C strategies," stated Sophia Chou, a specialist in organizational psychology at National Taiwan University.

7.   They Think "Consistency"

Humans are inherently inconsistent. That is why you cannot rely on your future self to carry out the plans you set today.

Assume you want to start eating a salad every day for lunch. You buy all the lettuce, tomatoes, onions, and cucumbers you need, but you forget you have a lunch meeting booked, so you miss lunch the next day because you're too busy. You probably won't eat that salad every day, and most of the components will spoil before you consume them.

Before making any goals-related decisions, effective people consider what can derail their efforts and how to work around them. Maintaining a consistent schedule and sticking to it can help you follow through.

8.   They Think "Meditation"

"The outcomes have been fantastic. Improved sleep. Relationships with spouses, children, and coworkers have improved. Some people who used to suffer from migraines no longer do. More productivity and creativity all around," said Oprah Winfrey about meditation.

It's no surprise that Oprah and other successful individuals, such as Russell Simmons, have made meditation a priority. Several meditation applications are available to help you get started with everyday meditation. You can get significant benefits in just five or ten minutes of your day.

9. They Think "Health is Wealth"

A healthy body and mind are prerequisites for success. Regular exercise and a good diet help you sleep better, enhance your immune system, raise your productivity, and improve your mental state.

Finding time to care for yourself might be difficult when you have a hectic lifestyle or travel frequently. Investing in a standing desk, going for a stroll during your lunch break, or performing easy exercises at your office are all excellent methods to establish an exercise routine.

Eating in moderation and avoiding cheap, greasy fast meals will help you eat a more balanced diet.

10. They Think "Leisure"

While successful individuals are recognized for their hard work, they also recognize the need to relax and recharge. They are, after all, just human. They understand that there is more to life than simply a job. Successful individuals make a point of having fun in their life.

Whether it's disconnecting for the weekend to spend time with their spouse, coming home for supper every night, volunteering, reading, exercising, or working on a hobby, they always make time for something they love.

This chapter emphasized the importance of having the correct success mentality. Cultivating the correct success mentality is not enough to become one of the world's most successful individuals; you must also follow several guidelines that have helped great men become great. The next chapter focuses on the principles that have made highly successful people successful and excellent in life.

Chapter 2

Principles of Purposeful Leadership

"The greatest leader is not necessarily the one who does the greatest things. He is the one that gets the people to do the greatest things." – Ronald Reagan

P urposeful leadership may be roughly defined as having strong values and principles for a team, paired with an ethical attitude and devotion to all key stakeholders or consumers.

Organizations' priorities have moved drastically in recent years, shifting

from a pure emphasis on the bottom line to a more holistic strategy that includes a movement toward purpose, people, and profit. Part of this shift stems from dissatisfaction with traditional short-term thinking that caused prior recessions, such as the 2008 financial crisis. However, worker priorities have shifted beyond only their monetary balance. One of the fundamental secrets of the world's successful individuals is purposeful leadership. Purposeful leadership may be roughly defined as having strong principles and ideals for a team, paired with an ethical attitude and devotion to all key stakeholders or consumers. Growing up,

11

I assumed that effective leaders had to figure out all the solutions independently. Being brilliant and ensuring everyone else knew it appeared to be their most notable characteristic. The greatest schools, it was assumed, would lead to the best employment, which would generate the best leaders. Professional success was measured by power, fame, glory, and money. Early in my career, I admired notable corporate executives like GE's Jack Welch for his intelligence, strategic insight, and hard-charging attitude. They were seen as infallible geniuses, creating a cult-like following. Purposeful leadership is defined as leadership that is motivated by a clear and compelling goal. Bardwick states, "Purposeful leadership is the process of aligning people and resources around a shared sense of purpose, creating a culture of meaning and belonging, and catalyzing action to achieve a better future." According to Kouzes and Posner, purposeful leadership involves "the power to create a shared vision and a sense of purpose that motivates and inspires others to achieve outstanding results." A purpose that is explicit and persuasive can inspire and motivate those around them. They are frequently led by honorable personal ideals that foster a healthy work atmosphere.

In this chapter, we'll go over these topics in further depth and look at some guiding principles for being a purposeful leader.

Purposeful Leadership's Fundamental Principles

The world's most successful leaders are deliberate leaders. They didn't get to the top by accident or chance. They were focused and determined. Here, I will demonstrate the basic tenets that drive purposeful leaders, what separates them from regular individuals, and how you may incorporate these characteristics into your everyday life to become a purposeful leader.

- **They understand their purpose in life:** Leaders with a sense of purpose know why they are here. They know exactly what they want to accomplish in life. They realized they weren't here by chance. According to Tony Robbins, "The only thing that will truly satisfy you is to live your life in alignment with your purpose." What is your motivation? What will people remember you for? Be honest in your personal, accurate appraisal of your strengths and flaws. Certainly, your mission cannot be found in your flaws. Accept your flaws with grace, but pursue your talents with zeal. Develop your strengths deliberately, intentionally, and consistently. Finding one's life purpose might be difficult, but it is worth pursuing. When you know your purpose, you will live a meaningful and rewarding life. Life's purpose generates life meaning. It's important to remember that discovering your life's purpose is a journey, not an event. It requires time, thought, and work. Regardless, get started.

- **They align their mission with honorable leadership values:** Lee Ellis cultivated certain characteristics of respectable leadership qualities. According to him, leaders demonstrate honorable principles by telling the truth even when it is tough, treating people with dignity and respect, keeping their word and commitments, being ethical in all their dealings, and acting properly and accountably, among other things. Establish your principles and begin living your life by them. Following the establishment of your values, you should pursue your purpose in a manner compatible with your values. Living according to your values may influence you as a person, your team, and the business as a whole. The most significant aspects of your life are your values. They are worth fighting for.

- **They live their purpose:** People who live their purpose live it every day. Purpose includes not just your words but also your actions and relationships with others. Roll up your sleeves and get something done every day. Growth occurs in little steps and is sustained over time. There is strength in doing something modest regularly since it may lead to great improvements over time. When you accomplish something tiny every day, you get momentum and find it simpler to keep going. You can make a difference even if you just have a few minutes each day. For example, you could get up early every day and write something tiny. That "something small" written every day will eventually become a book.

- **They communicate their purpose:** Another thing that purposeful leaders do is share their vision, aspirations, and purpose with those who share their values. Start Sharing information about your purpose with others to attract others who share your values. Every goal necessitates the presence of goal enablers. There is strength in articulating your objective to others. When your purpose is articulated, it may help you connect with others on a deeper level, encourage them to take action, and help you achieve your goals. It is critical to be clear about your goal so that you may express it to others in an honest and motivating manner. As a result, leaders should not hesitate to explain their mission to the rest of the world. Communicating your purpose is a powerful technique for connecting with others, inspiring them to act, and achieving your goals.

- **They Empower People:** By empowering followers, purposeful leaders develop more purposeful leaders, not followers. Make an effort to empower everyone in your immediate vicinity. The key to realizing your mission is to empower others. Build others and allow them to discover their purpose as an extension of your own. When you empower people, you are not only assisting them in achieving their goals but also in living meaningful lives. People who feel empowered are more likely to be interested in their jobs, more creative, and more productive. They are also more likely to be content with their life. They, in turn, will empower others. Purpose creates purpose. Purpose spreads like wildfire.

- **They foster a purpose-driven culture:** Purposeful executives understand how their job contributes to the organization's success and are driven to achieve their best. This will ensure the long-term viability of the company's mission, values, and vision. A purpose-driven culture is one in which workers feel linked to the company's mission and values. Long-term values and relationships are imprinted in established purpose-driven cultures, which are required for organizational longevity. Aside from being satisfied with their job, other advantages of developing a culture of purpose include having workers who are more likely to be engaged and productive and more inclined to stay with the organization. Creating a purpose-driven culture requires time and effort. It is, however, one of the most significant things a firm can do to enhance its performance and recruit and retain top people. According to Richard Branson, "A culture of purpose is about creating a company that is truly human."

One of the most significant leadership styles leaders may utilize to alter companies, corporations, and communities is purposeful leadership. They accomplish this by fostering a healthy and productive work atmosphere in which employees may maximize their innate creativity and human potential. In other words, intentional leaders can get the most out of their employees. Unsurprisingly, Ronald Reagan, the 40th President of the United States, observed, "The greatest leader is not always the one who accomplishes the most, he is the one who inspires others to accomplish extraordinary things."

Purposeful Leadership Foundational Integrity

Dwight D. Eisenhower once said, "There is no question that integrity is the most important trait for a leader." Without it, no true success is conceivable, whether on a gang, a football field, in the army, or in an office. In this subtopic on leadership and purpose, we go into the heart of leadership success by delving into a crucial trait: Integrity. Let's go on a trip to discover the value of leading with integrity—a pillar of purposeful leadership.

Personal Leadership Development

Let me tell you an inspiring story about the transforming power of purpose-driven leadership. I met a competent professional, let's call her Sarah, a few years ago. Sarah had slowly ascended the business ladder, gaining acclaim for her abilities. But a recurring discomfort remained behind the layers of accomplishment—a sense that her work lacked a greater purpose.

Sarah's career took an unexpected turn when she attended a leadership course focused on a purpose. The introspective activities in the program revealed her inner desire to contribute meaningfully, generating an epiphany that kindled her leadership style. Sarah integrated her career activities with her love for sustainability with renewed clarity.

She accomplished this by advocating environmentally friendly projects inside her firm. In doing so, Sarah re-energized her sense of purpose while leaving a lasting impression on the company's culture.

Integrity: The Foundation of Leadership

Integrity is the unshakable North Star in the world of leadership. Even in the most turbulent times, uprightness is the attribute that keeps us fixed. Authentic leaders are founded on integrity—a dedication to supporting ethical principles and moral ideals in all circumstances. This dedication is the foundation for trust and respect, upon which we establish meaningful connections and successful leadership.

Here are four strategies for maintaining integrity in your leadership journey:

1. **Consistent values:** Define your key beliefs clearly and ensure they are consistent with your leadership behaviors. The consistency between your stated principles and actions builds authenticity and trust among your team members.

2. **Open and Honest Communication:** Be open and honest in your conversations. Share your team's triumphs and difficulties, indicating your willingness to accept responsibility for your actions.

3. **Making Ethical Decisions:** When faced with difficult decisions, let your moral compass lead you to favor the greater good. And make judgments that demonstrate your dedication to justice and honesty.

4. **Lead by Example:** Set the example for honesty by demonstrating the conduct you demand from your team. When your actions match your words, you promote an integrity culture throughout your firm.

When purpose and integrity are harmoniously intertwined, authentic leadership thrives. Purpose pushes us ahead, pouring significant meaning into our activities, while integrity serves as an unshakeable guide, ensuring our path remains consistent with our beliefs.

Visionary Framework: Principles for Long-Term Success

What do I aspire to become when I grow up? It's a question I've been thinking about for more than a decade. That's exactly as it should be. We are always evolving. Realizing your full human potential takes a lifetime; the path never stops. So, envision, visualize, and design your way into the future. Consider the long term and dream large. Here are three questions you should ask yourself regularly:

1. What are my long-term targets? In five, ten, or twenty years, where do I see myself?

2. What kind of legacy do I want to leave behind once I die?

3. What would I regret not having accomplished when I retire?

Evaluating and implementing fresh ideas into your long-term vision can help you enhance your knowledge of your principles and make better short-term decisions.

When people fail to see their long-term prospects, it is typically due to one of two factors.

The first is what I refer to as **option paralysis**. The truth is that we live in incredibly remarkable times. Never before have so many options been readily available to so many of us. The choices force us to realize that our potential and possibilities are boundless. It implies that we must confront the truth of our freedom. We have complete freedom to pick EXACTLY what we want from a limitless array of employment alternatives.

It is difficult for humans to pick between three or four possibilities, let alone an unfathomable infinite of options. Understanding your values isn't much assistance because the things you care about and enjoy correlate with a bewildering assortment of occupations, positions, businesses, and sectors. Add to that the dread of making the incorrect decision, and you have a recipe for existential anguish - a continual sense of concern that you aren't all that you could be, and it's completely your own.

The second reason people fail to see the big picture is what I call **Short Term Myopia.** This indicates that your tastes are tied to where you are right now, and you can only envisage yourself one or two steps away. Perhaps you're an accountant who enjoys working with numbers but finds accounting tedious. So, you know you want to leave accounting, but it might be difficult to properly remove yourself from the past and see a truly new future that motivates you. Again, this is just human nature. Our thoughts are constantly conditioned by what we see and know, and it might be difficult to set them aside to construct a fresh vision.

When developing a long-term vision, the solutions to each issue are the same: disregard reality and dream large. Here is one method that will enable you to do so:

- Set aside one hour of undisturbed time for yourself.

- Find a quiet, comfortable area to sit and unwind.

- If you know how to meditate for a few minutes, simply sit for 10 minutes and listen to your breathing. Take note of the other sounds in the room. Simply observe calmly.

- Then ask yourself, "What would I do with my life if I could do anything?"

- Pay attention to your mind as it wanders; some images may be vivid and detailed, while others will be vague and fuzzy. Some will elicit powerful emotions and provide a burst of energy.

- Take notes as you observe items you wish to remember. Don't restrain yourself; simply write out whatever comes to mind. Pay special attention to the ones that make you feel energized and uplifted.
- Then return to your imagination.
- Repeat for an hour or until you run out of ideas.

It is entirely up to you what you do with your notes. You may go back over them immediately and try to form them into a definite image of your future. You may go back and see what new thoughts they spark. You might repeat this practice weekly or monthly to see what emerges as your path to achieving your goals.

Consider your long-term aim to be the North Star for a sailor. He'll never get there exactly, but it'll always let him know whether he's on the right track. A long-term vision's objective is to inspire you and help you make excellent decisions in the present. No matter how detailed your vision is, it will almost certainly emerge differently than you see it - most likely in a way that exceeds what you believed was conceivable when you dreamed it up.

So, resist the need to transform your long-term vision into a specific objective and create a thorough strategy to attain it. Instead, keep it in front of you as the inspiring destination you aim for, and then make wise short-term decisions to get you there.

Transparent Leadership: Building Trust

To be great and successful, you must live a transparent life. Transparency is being open, honest, and responsible in activities and decisions. As a leader, establishing trust with your followers, colleagues, and stakeholders is critical. Trust is the bedrock of any successful relationship, including those in business. To succeed in a company, you must first build trust with your employees or team members. Open and honest communication, stability, and dependability establish trust. People are more likely to feel appreciated and driven when they trust their leaders.

A leader who is open and honest with his or her followers fosters a climate of trust and open communication. Transparency also contributes to credibility since people perceive their leader as truthful. A transparent leader is also more likely to recognize and accept responsibility for mistakes, fostering an accountability and continuous improvement culture.

A lack of trust and openness in leadership can result in issues such as low morale, lower production, and high turnover rates. People may be less eager to take chances, provide feedback, or make recommendations if they do not trust you as a leader, which can discourage creativity and impede growth. Furthermore, a lack of openness can lead to confusion and ambiguity, rumors, conjectures, and distrust among individuals.

There are various procedures that must be followed to foster trust and openness in leadership:

- Leaders must always speak freely and honestly with the people they govern, especially when the news is bad.
- Leaders must establish clear expectations and offer frequent feedback to ensure their followers understand their duties and responsibilities.
- Leaders should provide a good example for their followers by modeling the conduct they anticipate.
- Leaders must accept responsibility for their actions and judgments, admit mistakes, and try to fix them.

Be Honest About Your Feelings and Ideals.

As a leader, genuinely and respectfully sharing your feelings and beliefs with your team and other stakeholders is critical to enabling people to connect with you. To be honest about your emotions and values, to display empathy and compassion, to discuss your feelings appropriately, to demonstrate your values through your actions and decisions, and to appreciate the diversity of emotions and values on your team. This will build an inclusive and respectful atmosphere.

How to Be Honest About Your Mistakes and Failures

As a leader, you must accept, learn from, and share your mistakes and shortcomings with your team and other stakeholders. This demonstrates that you are human, modest, and eager to accept responsibility and improve. The first step is to admit and apologize for your faults. Seek comments and guidance from your team and other stakeholders, as well as undertake corrective and preventative steps to avoid repeating the same mistakes. Encourage your staff and other stakeholders to disclose their setbacks and errors so that you can assist them in overcoming them. You may assure transparency regarding your faults and failures by doing so.

How to Overcome Transparency Challenges

Being open and honest as a leader is not always easy. Coping with sensitive or secret material, balancing the quantity and frequency of information you provide, coping with unfavorable reactions, and preserving your credibility while being open and vulnerable are all possible problems. To overcome these obstacles, you should adhere to applicable information-sharing laws and procedures, prioritize and personalize the information you offer, respond to unfavorable emotions with respect and curiosity, and highlight your strengths and successes while being honest and modest.

Transparency and trust are critical components of good leadership. As a leader, you must develop trust and communicate freely and honestly with your team members to foster a culture of responsibility, inspiration, and productivity.

People are more inclined to work hard and contribute to your achievement if they trust you as a leader and understand your tasks and responsibilities. As a result, to achieve long-term success, you must emphasize trust and honesty in your dealings with others.

In the next chapter, I will walk you through the many strategic thinking techniques the world's successful people use. We'll talk about what you need to do to start thinking strategically about changing your life and being great tomorrow.

Chapter 3

Strategic Thinking for Success

"Success doesn't necessarily come from breakthrough innovation but from flawless execution. A great strategy alone won't win a game or a battle; the win comes from basic blocking and tackling." – Naveen Jain

C onsider yourself to be seated across a chessboard from a powerful opponent. Your heart is racing as you consider your next step. A bad decision might cost you the game, yet each planned move brings you closer to victory. Life, like chess, needs strategic thinking to manage its hurdles and capitalize on chances. Strategic thinking is the key to realizing your full potential and attaining success in your personal and professional lives. Strategic thinking, in its most basic form, is the capacity to prepare for the future.

It is the ability to plan, and generate ideas to deal with changing circumstances while also considering the numerous problems that lie ahead.

In this chapter, we'll dig into the area of strategic thinking, drawing inspiration from the ideas and public speeches of great, successful leaders and providing insights to help you improve your decision-making abilities. Are you prepared to go on this intellectual adventure? Then, let's get started!

The Essence of Strategy

It is critical to grasp what strategy is before you can become a strategic thinker. Strategy is derived from the Greek word "strategos," which means "generalship" or "art of the general," and refers to the high-level planning and decision-making that drives success in a specific setting. In essence, strategy is about making educated decisions amid uncertainty, competition, and resource restrictions to accomplish desired objectives.

What exactly is Strategic Thinking?

Strategic thinking is a deliberate and reasonable thought process that focuses on examining crucial elements and variables that will impact a company's, team's, or individual's long-term performance.

Strategic thinking entails anticipating risks and weaknesses to avoid and opportunities to pursue. Strategic thinking and analysis, in the end, result in a clear set of objectives, strategies, and fresh ideas essential to survive and grow in a competitive, changing world. This type of thinking must consider economic realities, market dynamics, and available resources.

Research, analytical thinking, inventiveness, problem-solving abilities, communication and leadership skills, and decisiveness are all required for strategic thinking.

Why is Strategic Thinking Important for Effective Leadership?

Strategic thinking is essential for good leadership because it helps leaders anticipate changes, prioritize activities, and efficiently allocate resources, resulting in innovation and a competitive edge in their world. On the other hand, leaders who do not think strategically risk making short-sighted judgments that have a detrimental influence on their world in the long run. Leaders must emphasize strategic thought and build their talents via deliberate effort and practice to avoid these mistakes.

The Foundations of Strategic Thinking

Strategic thinking isn't just one talent; it's a multidimensional mental framework built on four basic important pillars:

1. **Vision:** To think strategically, you must first comprehend your intended end state or target. This vision directs your actions, ensuring they align with your long-term objectives.

2. **Analysis:** Strategic thinkers are skilled at obtaining, understanding, and analyzing data. They investigate their surroundings, find trends, and spot patterns that may influence their pursuit of their goal.

3. **Planning:** Strategic thinkers create a road plan for success based on a clear vision and educated analysis. They examine various possibilities, balance the risks and benefits, and allocate resources to maximize their chances of success.

4. **Execution:** Finally, strategic thought leads to action. Strategic thinkers execute their plans precisely, evaluate progress, and change as needed to guarantee their vision is realized.

Developing Your Strategic Thinking Capabilities

Becoming a strategic thinker requires ongoing development and self-improvement. Here are some concrete strategies you may take to improve your strategic thinking abilities:

- **Encourage curiosity:** Be curious and ask questions. Seek to comprehend the "why" of decisions and the circumstances in which they are made. Curiosity feeds creativity, allowing you to go beyond the apparent and develop new solutions to challenges.

- **Broaden your horizons:** Experiment with new experiences, ideas, and points of view. Read widely, participate in discussions, and attend conferences or seminars. Broadening your viewpoint can assist you in recognizing patterns and making connections that others may miss.

- **Use scenario planning:** Visualize many future situations and consider how they could affect your goals regularly. This activity will not only assist you in preparing for unexpected obstacles, but it will also improve your ability to detect opportunities and hazards.

- **Observe and learn from others:** Pay attention to and learn from the strategic thinkers around you. Identify role models, seek mentoring, and converse with individuals who inspire you.

Imitating their habits and thought processes can help you become a strategic thinker faster.

- **Reflect and refine:** Strategic thinking is a talent that must be constantly refined and refined. Make time to reflect on your decisions, evaluate their results, and discover opportunities for improvement. With this self-awareness, you can develop and adapt throughout time.

Strategic thinking is a significant tool in pursuing personal and professional success. You will be better able to negotiate the intricacies of life and capture opportunities if you comprehend the essence of strategy, master the pillars of strategic thinking, and continually hone your talents.

Leadership Agility in Dynamic Environments

Adaptability is an essential attribute for leaders and successful individuals alike in today's fast-paced, ever-changing environment. Leadership agility is the capacity to foresee change, respond quickly, pivot, and exploit opportunities. The world is changing very quickly. Technological improvements, market dynamics, client preferences, and even worldwide pandemics contribute to an unpredictable corporate picture. In such a climate, inflexible leadership styles might limit a company's capacity to change. Agile leaders, on the other hand, tend to keep their teams and organizations ahead of the curve, capitalize on shifts early, and establish a distinct competitive edge.

The benefits of agile working methods

Improved adaptability: When individuals adapt quickly and successfully to their environment, they are better equipped to respond to changing market dynamics, client requirements, and internal objectives. As a result, firms will be able to keep ahead of the competition and seize new opportunities as they occur.

- **Improved collaboration:** Workplace agility inspires efforts to interact and communicate, breaking invisible barriers and boosting cross-functional teamwork. This collaborative setting promotes information exchange, innovation, and a sense of community.

- **Continuous improvement:** It is unavoidable for a group of agile employees to aspire to be even better via information exchange, creativity, and a sense of collective responsibility. Teams evaluate their performance, identify areas for improvement, and gradually make changes to build a culture of learning and growth.

Leadership agility is more important than ever, and here's how you develop it:

1. **Adopt a Growth Mindset:** Agile leaders perceive problems as opportunities to learn and progress rather than threats. They are receptive to feedback, do not fear making errors, and always look for ways to better themselves and their teams.

2. **Accept Change:** While change might be difficult, it is frequently a driver of creativity. Agile leaders embrace rather than fight

32

change. They inspire their colleagues to follow suit, fostering an organizational culture that views change as an opportunity.

3. **Promote Diversity and Inclusion:** Diverse teams contribute a broader range of viewpoints and ideas, which fosters creativity and innovation. Agile leaders value and promote diversity, creating a welcoming workplace where all perspectives are heard.

4. **Make Continuous Learning a Priority:** The world is changing rapidly, and what worked yesterday may not work today. Agile leaders encourage constant learning and growth for themselves and their teams to be at the forefront of their industry.

5. **Empower Your Team:** Agile leaders recognize the value of a highly engaged and empowered team. They successfully delegate, foster trust, and encourage autonomy, allowing team members to take ownership and make swift choices.

Leadership agility is about being resilient, adaptive, flexible, and open to change, not moving rapidly. It is about anticipating and preparing for the future while remaining present. It is about understanding that while striving for perfection is great, the goal is to make constant improvement. Cultivating leadership agility is a continuous effort that may contribute to long-term success, especially in a dynamic and unpredictable corporate environment.

Innovative Problem-Solving Techniques

The capacity to innovate and solve issues creatively has emerged as a key talent for individuals, corporations, and societies alike in today's quickly expanding world, where challenges are becoming increasingly complex and dynamic. Innovation is the driving force behind progress, pulling us ahead in various fields, including technology and science, as well as commercial and social growth. With as many difficulties as we all confront in our jobs and lives; it appears that there is never enough time to tackle them all without encountering some difficulty along the road. Problems pile up so quickly that we find ourselves using shortcuts to momentarily relieve tension points - so we can move on to the next one. In the process, we fail to tackle the heart of each problem we face; as a result, we are always locked in a never-ending loop that makes finding true answers impossible. Does this sound familiar?

The core of what leaders exist to accomplish is to solve problems. The purpose of leaders is to limit the occurrence of issues, which means we must be bold enough to confront them before circumstances force our hand. We must be tenacious in building and sustaining momentum for the organization and the individuals we serve. However, in the office, we encounter people who complicate issues through corporate politicking, self-promotion, power manoeuvres and ploys, and jealousy. Silos, a lack of finances and resources, and a variety of other unforeseeable events or conditions also make it difficult for workers to be productive.

When a competitor unexpectedly converts a long-standing client, establishes a new industry relationship, or launches a new product, brand, or corporate strategy, it challenges us. Mergers and acquisitions keep us on our toes and divert our attention away from current issues by creating new ones.

One of the most famous twentieth-century philosophers of science, Karl Popper, once said, "All life is problem-solving." I've long maintained that the finest leaders are the best problem solvers. They have the patience to take a step back and look at the situation from a different angle, using extended observation and circular vision. They can look around, beneath, and beyond the issue. They perceive far beyond what is visible. The most effective leaders view situations through an opportunity lens. Leaders who lack this insight approach problems with linear vision, seeing just the problem in front of them and ignoring the options that exist inside the problem. As a result, they never perceive the problem in its entirety, and it may serve as a catalyst for improving current best practices, protocols, and standard operating procedures for developing and competing in the marketplace. They fail to see that, in the end, all issues are the same - they are only packaged differently.

A leader never sees an issue as a distraction but as a strategic facilitator for continual progress and previously undiscovered opportunities. Whether you are a leader for a huge organization, a small business owner, or an aspiring leader, here are the four most effective problem-solving strategies great leaders use.

- **Open and Honest Communication**

Problem resolution necessitates open communication in which everyone's concerns and points of view may be openly shared. I've seen firsthand how difficult it is to resolve a problem promptly when individuals don't speak out.

Yes, communication is an absolute must. That is why, when persons concerned with the problem prefer not to express themselves for fear of jeopardizing their employment and/or exposing their own or someone else's misconduct, the approach to problem-solving becomes similar to a treasure hunt. Effective issue-solving communication occurs due to a leader's ability to enable an open discussion among individuals who trust her intentions and believe they are in a secure atmosphere to communicate why they believe the problem occurred and specific solutions.

Once all voices have been heard and all points of view have been considered, the leader (together with her team) may chart out a route toward a feasible and sustainable solution. As basic as communication may seem, never assume that individuals are comfortable communicating their true feelings. A leader must trust herself and her instincts enough to push the team until responsibility is equitably imposed and a solution is discovered.

- **Dismantle Silos**

Transparent communication necessitates breaking down silos and enabling a boundary-less company with a culture centered on the improvement of a healthy whole. Unnecessary silos attract hidden motives rather than effective cross-functional collaboration and problem-solving.

Most workplace problems are the result of organizational silos, which is why many of them never get fixed. This is why today's modern workplace must embrace an entrepreneurial spirit in which workers may freely traverse and cross-collaborate to connect the problem-solving dots, in which everyone can be a passionate explorer who understands their workplace dot and its intersections. You have a much better understanding of your area of influence when you know your workplace. This is nearly tough to assess when you work in silos that may prevent you from having any effect at all.

Problem resolution is more challenging in a siloed company since you are more likely to deal with self-promoters rather than team players nurtured by a cross-functional setting. When you work in a segregated atmosphere where everyone wants to be a star, it becomes more impossible to contribute to the improvement of anything or anybody. Problem resolution becomes a frustrating endeavor at this point.

Breaking down divisions enables leaders to more readily engage their followers or employees in getting their hands dirty and working together to solve challenges. It becomes less about corporate politics and more about finding answers and strengthening the planet.

- **Open-minded People**

People must be open-minded to break down silos and communication obstacles. Finally, problem-solving is about individuals coming together to improve the world and the people it serves. As a result, if you're trapped dealing with closed-minded people, effective problem-solving becomes a lengthy and twisting path of suffering.

Many people in the office are causing unneeded commotion to keep their inefficiencies hidden. These sorts of people (loafers and leeches) make it harder to solve problems because they slow down the process to make themselves appear more significant. Discover the lifters and high-potential leaders within the sphere to discover the advantages of being open-minded and how this eventually leads to greater creativity and initiative. Open-minded individuals look beyond the obvious facts in front of them and consider risk to be their greatest friend. They confront issues front-on and get down to promoting development and innovation. Close-minded individuals twist events to make them more about themselves and less about what it takes to turn a problem into a fresh opportunity.

With this explanation in mind, pay close attention to the conduct of others the next time you encounter a real situation.

- **A Firm Foundation Strategy**

Change without strategy is only replacement, not evolution. To tackle any problem, a strong approach must be applied. Many leaders try to analyze an issue rather than uncover the solution that resides inside the problem itself.

Effective problem-solving leaders always know how to assemble the proper people, resources, money, and expertise from previous experiences. They motivate individuals to improve by making problem-solving a collaborative process; for them, it's an opportunity to bring people closer together. I've always felt that you don't know a person's full ability and character until you see how they handle difficulties.

Effective leaders connect the links and create a feasible course of action ahead of time. They have a plan that will serve as the framework for addressing and handling the situation. They plan for the unexpected and leverage their people's capabilities to ensure the approach leads to a long-term solution.

When it comes to issue resolution, never fire from the hip. Avoid making assumptions. Allow yourself adequate time to examine the issue and the opportunity that each challenge brings. Make the issue-solving process more efficient by acknowledging that each problem has subtleties that may necessitate a unique approach to a feasible solution.

When problem-solving becomes a smooth process that allows individuals and the company to develop and improve, you know you have exceptional leadership in your business. If solving problems causes turmoil, you may be lacking in leadership.

The biggest facilitator of development and opportunity is problem resolution. This is why they say failure is the best teacher in business and life. Be a leader who demonstrates maturity, acts bravely, and demands responsibility. Each of these classes can assist you in becoming a master problem solver. Every event teaches us something new. Accept problem-solving and all of the hidden gems it symbolizes.

You have learned in this chapter that the capacity to think strategically is a significant tool in pursuing personal and professional success. You will be better able to negotiate the intricacies of life and capture opportunities if you comprehend the essence of strategy and agile leadership, master the pillars of strategic thinking, and continually develop your problem-solving abilities.

In the next chapter, I will reveal the communication tactics and styles used by highly successful leaders to transmit their ideas convincingly and develop strong connections, as well as how to follow in their footsteps.

Chapter 4

Effective Communication Strategies

"Effective leadership is not about making speeches or being liked; leadership is defined by results, not attributes. And the most effective communication tool is your attitude." – Peter Drucker

A successful leader must be able to communicate effectively. Communication and leadership are inextricably linked. To accomplish achievements via others, you must be a great communicator in numerous connections at the company level, in communities and groups, and occasionally on a worldwide scale.

Leaders must think, explain ideas, and communicate with various audiences. They must also deal with the quick flow of information within the business and between consumers, partners, vendors, and other stakeholders and influencers.

Importance of Communication in Leadership

Communication is more involved than the fundamental mechanics of giving and receiving information. When leaders harness the capacity to communicate successfully, they can convey critical facts quickly and precisely.

One of a leader's most critical qualities is the ability to communicate. Effective communication requires both purpose and intention. You must know when and how to communicate, as well as which mode is best for your audience. Leaders must thrive at communication in all modalities, whether they are writing, conversing, presenting, or facilitating. It is the only method to address people's requirements while facilitating vital interpersonal interactions. Effective communication is the bedrock of effective leadership. It promotes connections, trust, and a common vision. The capacity to communicate, with influence, and with effect is the key to a leader's success. Through my experience working with multiple highly successful leaders, I've established a framework encompassing the behaviors and characteristics that make them outstanding communicators. Curiosity, Listening, Empathy, Awareness, Respect, Presence, Authenticity, Communicating with Power and Purpose, and Enabling make up the CLEAR PACE framework. Scientific data support these behaviors and characteristics and may be developed using practical methods.

- **Curiosity: Developing A Desire for Knowledge**

  Curiosity drives leaders to aggressively strive to comprehend their team members and stakeholders. They pose provocative inquiries, eliciting ideas and viewpoints that may go unnoticed. Curiosity has been found in studies to improve learning, engagement, and problem-solving skills. Curiosity fosters an environment in which ideas flow freely, and cooperation thrives.

- **Opening Hearts and Minds Through Listening**

  Listening is fully knowing people via attentive listening and sensitivity to subtle indications. Listening fosters better relationships and more effective conflict resolution by creating a secure environment where individuals feel heard and respected. Leaders create trust in their teams by refining their listening abilities.

- **Empathy: Displaying Concern and Care**

  Empathic leaders show real concern for the well-being of their team members. Empathy improves comprehension, builds relationships, and boosts team members engagement. Empathetic leaders are more successful at motivating and inspiring their staff, resulting in better levels of productivity and creativity.

- **Mindfulness and the Power of Awareness**

  Self-conscious leaders are more aware of their emotions and how they affect others. Mindfulness assists leaders in navigating difficult circumstances with grace and poise. They can successfully analyze and respond to the requirements of their team and change their communication technique based on the context and the needs of their audience by being present in the moment, ensuring that their message resonates.

- **Respect is the Foundation of Trust.**

  Respectful leaders provide an open and collaborative workplace. They respect other points of view and treat people with dignity, resulting in better levels of team engagement, loyalty, and dedication. Leaders motivate people to reciprocate by exhibiting respect and engaging in open and honest discourse.

- **Authenticity as a Means of Commanding Attention**

  Leaders who are involved in the present, exhibiting confidence and sincerity, fascinate and make an indelible impact on their audience. According to research, leaders who portray a strong presence are seen as more trustworthy, persuasive, and influential. Leaders may successfully transmit their messages and motivate action by utilizing the power of presence.

- **Genuine Connections Require Authenticity**

  Authenticity is the link between leaders and their teams. Genuine leaders are faithful to their ideals and principles. They build a profound connection by sharing their stories, weaknesses, and accomplishments and inspire others to do the same. According to research, authentic leaders are more likely to instill trust, loyalty, and dedication in their teams.

Making Words Count in Powerful Communication

To communicate effectively, you must have both purpose and clarity. Leaders who speak with strength and purpose carefully pick their words, ensuring that their message is successfully conveyed. They recognize the significance of adapting their communication approach to various audiences and situations. According to research, leaders who communicate inspire trust, improve team performance, and achieve corporate goals.

Enabling: Providing Opportunities for Others to Succeed

Capable leaders enable their teams to reach their maximum potential. Leaders encourage their team members to express themselves by creating a psychologically secure atmosphere, fostering open communication, and offering constructive criticism. Leaders may also cultivate their teams' abilities by promoting a culture of continual learning and growth, which leads to increased productivity and creativity.

Useful Tools for Improving Your Communication

1. **Promote a Learning Mentality and Varied Perspectives:** Provide chances for team members to share their thoughts and experiences, while encouraging curiosity and investigation.
2. **Engage in Active and Thoughtful Listening:** Pay attention to the speaker and refrain from interrupting. To guarantee complete

comprehension, summarize and paraphrase what the speaker has said. This shows that you care and invites more conversation.

3. **Improve Your Perspective-Taking Skills:** By putting yourself in the shoes of others and attempting to comprehend their ideas, feelings, and experiences. This promotes the development of empathy and compassion.

4. **Show Empathy with Gestures:** To demonstrate care and concern, offer support and encouragement, acknowledge feelings, and validate others' experiences.

5. **Promote Self-reflection:** Make time for introspection and self-evaluation regularly.

6. **Seek Feedback:** Seek feedback actively to learn how your communication style is viewed.

7. **Set an example** of polite communication within the team.

8. **Practice Mindfulness** by focusing on the conversation at hand and limiting distractions.

9. **Use Good Body Language:** Maintain an open posture, create adequate eye contact, and communicate involvement with facial expressions and movements.

10. **Be Willing to Be Vulnerable:** Share personal tales and experiences that illustrate your sincerity and help others to connect with you on a deeper level.

11. **Use Storytelling Approaches** to explain crucial ideas, engage emotions, and make your message more remembered.

12. **Establish a Safe Environment:** Create an environment where people feel comfortable sharing their opinions and ideas without fear of being judged or retaliated against.

By integrating these tactics, leaders may improve their communication efficacy and create a good, engaging atmosphere for their teams. Learning to communicate effectively is a journey that involves dedication, practice, and self-reflection. As a leader, you may better unleash your full potential in motivating people, developing strong connections, and leading with clarity, influence, and impact by adopting the **CLEAR PACE** framework.

Communication Technology Challenges

However, modern communication technologies pose certain leadership issues. They can, for example, provide an overflow of information and diversions, such as too many messages and notifications. They can also decrease face-to-face engagement and human connection, resulting in a loss of emotional signals, rapport, and trust. Furthermore, technological concerns, privacy breaches, and cyberattacks can raise complexity and danger. Finally, they necessitate acquiring new skills and competencies such as digital literacy, etiquette, and culture.

Best methods for communicating with technology

To make the most of communication technology and overcome hurdles, leaders must establish clear communication objectives and expectations, such as purpose, frequency, and format. They must select the most appropriate and effective technology for each occasion and audience, such as video conferencing for brainstorming and emailing for updates. They should also balance the use of new technology with more conventional techniques such as phone calls, meetings, and human visits. Finally, they should track and assess the effectiveness and consequences of communication, such as feedback, performance, and satisfaction.

Examples of How to Use Communication Technology

Here are some examples from various industries and circumstances of how leaders are putting modern communication technology to use in practice. For example, a multinational corporation uses a cloud-based platform to connect its workers, customers, and partners while providing training, support, and innovation possibilities. A nonprofit organization also uses a podcast to convey its stories, values, and influence to its supporters, volunteers, and beneficiaries. In addition, a government agency uses a dashboard to track and communicate its progress, issues, and accomplishments to stakeholders and the general public. Finally, a small firm uses video conferencing software to provide online workshops, consultations, and coaching sessions with its customers.

Communication Technology Developments in the Future

Leaders must be aware of and prepared for new communication technologies that are continually growing and emerging as they provide new opportunities and problems. Chatbots, voice assistants, and sentiment analysis are examples of how artificial intelligence (AI) and machine learning (ML) may automate and improve communication operations. Immersive and interactive communication experiences, such as simulations, demonstrations, and tours, may be created using augmented reality (AR) and virtual reality (VR). Blockchain and cryptocurrency may make contracts, payments, and donations more secure and transparent. Furthermore, the Internet of Things (IoT) and 5G can connect and communicate with various devices and networks, including sensors, cameras, and smart objects.

Power of Storytelling

Storytelling is a powerful tool for leaders who wish to inspire, motivate, and impact change in their teams, organizations, and stakeholders. It may help you express your vision, objectives, and goals and connect emotionally and rationally with your audience. Storytelling is more than merely entertaining or influencing others. It's also about making sense and understanding, which is especially important in times of uncertainty, complexity, and change. When you tell a tale, you ask your audience to accompany you on a trip where they may see the obstacles, possibilities, and solutions that you envision. You also explain how they may participate in the transformation and what rewards they might expect.

Storytelling may help you gain your audience's trust, credibility, and involvement and overcome resistance and objections. Ineffective workplace communication causes severe emotional and psychological harm, hurting productivity, morale, staff retention, and effectiveness. Fortunately, there is a way to make things different.

How can we encourage good communication that respects the speaker and the listener? How can we, as leaders, establish deeper relationships by appealing to emotions, goals, and values?

I'll show you a shockingly simple way to prevent poor communication. It has something to do with something we've been doing since the beginning. What was one of your early memories as a child?

Yes, you did tell stories! Here are six methods of using storytelling to persuade and inspire:

1. Define Your Objective.

Maintaining a clear purpose is critical while writing stories. The story should correspond to a point or message we want to express. Otherwise, our listeners may lose sight of or interest in the intended takeaway.

It might be as easy as stating, "Let's do this together" or "I believe in us." You may motivate your team to action by demonstrating that you are not just their leader but also a team member. Remember, a tale is about us, not just you or me.

Take, for example, Elon Musk, CEO of SpaceX. He was open about the odds of success as he prepared to send the Falcon Heavy rocket into orbit for the first time. Musk stated that there was a strong possibility the rocket might explode, causing the launch to fail. But he didn't allow the possibility of failure to stop him from trying. He said something along the lines of, "Let's give it a shot." In any case, it'll be a fantastic concert."

What's more, guess what? They were successful! They sent a Tesla Roadster into orbit around the sun using the most powerful rocket ever fired.

Remind your squad of the Falcon Heavy whenever they confront a difficult challenge. Tell them that no matter how difficult a task appears, giving it an attempt might result in success. Even if it doesn't, we learn, develop, and return stronger.

2. Create Emotional Bonds.

You're on the correct road if you've determined your aim, the endpoint of your narrative trip, and the direction you want to guide your audience. The first step in influencing and inspiring your audience has been taken. However, to reach our target, we require a propellant. Forging an emotional connection is the most powerful fuel for maximizing an individual's potential.

Steve Jobs did not merely reel off a list of technical features during the presentation of the iMac in 1998, the device destined to become the centerpiece of Apple's return. Instead, he woven a story. He described how the iMac was designed to be unlike any other computer on the market. It was created to look like a pleasant face with its brilliant colors, curves, and user-friendly design.

This story, this emotional connection to the goods, struck a chord with the audience. The iMac quickly became a smashing success for Apple, accounting for about half of the company's sales, illustrating the power of emotional connection in product marketing.

As leaders, we can use the same strategy to interact with our teams and stakeholders. We can build a shared sense of purpose and dedication by producing tales that strike an emotional chord, enabling success in any endeavor.

3. Accept Simplicity.

Storytelling does not have to be a maze of complex details. Instead, simplicity and clarity aid in smoothly transmitting our intended message, making it more understandable to our audience.

Let's go back to my favorite technology business, Apple. A good example of this is their "Think Different" initiative. Apple was competing with behemoths like IBM and Microsoft in the late 1990s. To differentiate themselves, they launched the "Think Different" campaign. Advertisements featured prominent inventors and intellectuals such as Albert Einstein, Mahatma Gandhi, and Martin Luther King Jr.

These advertisements did not tell difficult stories. They were just black-and-white photographs of these notable people, along with the message "Think Different." They produced an unforgettable impact despite their simplicity. They spoke to individuals who wanted a break from the routine, who sought the unique and imaginative. It encapsulated Apple's ethos: creativity, innovation, and nonconformity.

The idea is simple: simple tales combined with a clear message may be extremely powerful and effective. As leaders, we must aim for simplicity and clarity in our storytelling so that our intended message is simply understood and connected.

4. Check for Relevancy

When I went on my second foreign tour, I headed a team of 14 young businesspeople, many of whom had been labeled underachievers by their prior bosses. I was new, having recently transferred, and instead of adopting the prevalent preconceptions, I opted to listen, learn, and lead.

I interacted with each one individually, learning about their perspectives and motives. I shared my experiences, developed rapport, and earned trust. I convinced them they could be the top IT team in that area of operations. I, too, had been misjudged and called a failure because I had been misunderstood. But I began to thrive when someone put time and faith in me. I planned to do the same for my squad.

Leading entails both encouraging and inciting action. It doesn't need to be perfect.

5. Avoid Making Mistakes

You must have a critical and creative perspective and a commitment to learn and develop to avoid typical narrative blunders. Telling a dull or irrelevant tale that does not grab or maintain your audience's attention, one that is confused or inconsistent without a clear goal, message, or structure, or one that is self-centered or arrogant are all examples of faults. You should also avoid incorrect or overblown stories that do not represent reality or truth and may harm your reputation. To avoid making these mistakes, always test and modify your story before delivering it and get input from others.

6. Take Action.

Practice your storytelling abilities and apply them in various scenarios to reach a wide range of people. The more you practice, the better you'll get and the more confident you'll present your message. It is only through practice that you will be able to explore your memory for stories that are relevant to the circumstance.

You are both the author and the protagonist in this story about leadership and communication. So, tell an engaging tale that inspires connection, propels accomplishment, and leaves a lasting impression.

Emotional Intelligence in Communication

Team communication is essential for any leader, especially in today's complicated and varied workplaces. But how can you successfully connect with your team members or followers while simultaneously demonstrating emotional intelligence and leadership? In this section, we will look at some of the most important parts of team communication and how you can utilize them to foster trust, cooperation, and engagement among your team and those who look up to you as a leader.

What Exactly is Emotional Intelligence?

Emotional intelligence (EI) is the capacity to comprehend and control one's emotions and sympathize with and interact with people with diverse feelings, views, and backgrounds. EI is important for team communication since it helps you avoid disagreements, solve problems, and inspire your team members. EI also assists you in adapting to new circumstances and dealing with stress and ambiguity.

Emotional Intelligence Development

Emotional intelligence (EI) development necessitates continuous practice of the four primary components: self-awareness, self-regulation, social awareness, and social skills. Reflect on your emotions, strengths, limitations, and values to develop your EI. Set your objectives and standards, and learn to regulate your impulses and reactions. Pay attention to others' feelings, wants, and expectations, and be mindful of power dynamics and team politics. Use verbal and nonverbal clues to communicate effectively, confidently, and politely with others. Adapt your communication style to various audiences and scenarios. Collaborate with people to establish rapport and trust. Use tools like journaling, meditation, or personality tests to learn more about yourself and practices like breathing exercises or positive affirmations to relax. Seek out comments from others to help you improve your emotional intelligence.

Taking the Lead in Team Communication

To demonstrate leadership in team communication, you must employ various skills, techniques, and communication styles appropriate for your team's requirements, objectives, and difficulties. As a leader, you must establish and convey a clear and compelling vision and objective for your team, explaining why it is essential and how it matches the values and mission of the team. Furthermore, you should assign tasks and responsibilities to team members appropriate for their talents, interests, and potential while providing them with the required resources and assistance. You must also acknowledge and thank your team members for their accomplishments, contributions, and efforts. It's also critical to encourage and coach your team members when they experience hurdles or difficulties. Finally, you must model and encourage the values and behaviors you demand from your team members. This will build a good and effective team environment.

Emotional intelligence and leadership balance in team communication. The goal of balancing emotional intelligence and leadership in team communication is difficult yet necessary. It may be tough to balance being empathic and aggressive, helpful and demanding, and flexible and decisive. It's also critical to keep your emotions and needs in sync with those of your team members while avoiding being too emotional or distant. Here are some pointers to help you strike the appropriate balance: Know yourself and your team by conducting surveys, evaluations, or feedback sessions to obtain a better knowledge of your own emotional intelligence and leadership style, as well as the team's. Adapt yourself and your team to the situation, aim, and audience by adjusting your emotional intelligence and leadership style. You can employ coaching, mentoring, or training to assist your team members in doing the same. Check your emotional intelligence and leadership performance, as well as your team's performance regularly. Gather information via feedback, review, or reflection.

Successful leadership is built on effective communication. Leaders who grasp the art of communication may inspire, encourage, and direct their followers or teams to achieve common goals. Throughout this chapter, we have looked at several components of good communication, such as what communication is all about, how technology can be used in communication, and how leaders may use emotional intelligence in communication. We also reviewed the benefits of communication technologies in leadership and many instances and future communication technology developments that may benefit successful leadership.

In the next chapter, I will discuss how networking plays a significant part in the success of highly successful leaders and how you may utilize this practically and strategically to develop important professional relationships.

Let us begin our trip!

Chapter 5

The Power of Networking and Relationship Building

"Networking isn't about just connecting people. It's about connecting people with people, people with ideas, and people with opportunities." – Michele Jennae

Many of us associate networking with packed conference rooms filled with unpleasant small chats and one-sided interactions that eventually conclude with the exchange of business cards that end up in the bottom drawer.

However, the adage "it's not what you know, it's who you know" holds, and in today's fast-paced corporate environment, creating and keeping good professional connections is critical to success.

Networking, in particular, can be a tremendous tool for leaders, opening doors, creating possibilities, and fostering personal and professional growth.

In this chapter, I'll teach you how to create an effective network and, more crucially, how to keep meaningful relationships.

Creating a Support Network

During tough times, professional networks act as a support system. Surrounding oneself with others who share your work struggles and goals gives emotional support and encouragement. These relationships can aid in building resilience by reminding you that you are not alone.

Encourage Collaboration and Innovation

Networking promotes teamwork and innovation. When you interact with experts from other backgrounds, you open the door to cooperation and idea-sharing. Collaborative efforts not only result in inventive solutions but also boost your resilience by showcasing the strength of teamwork in overcoming problems.

Access to Mentorship and Guidance

Networking provides access to mentoring and direction from experienced professionals. A mentor who has been through the ups and downs of the working world may provide useful insights and advice. Mentors can help you navigate problems and develop resilience by sharing their experiences and skills.

Improving Communication Skills

Excellent communication skills are required for effective networking. Conversations with strangers may increase your confidence, communication skills, and capacity to develop connections with people. These abilities are critical for developing resilience because they allow you to handle disputes and overcome setbacks.

Increasing Your Influence

Networking helps you broaden your influence area and establish yourself as a useful conduit in your field. You develop resilience by becoming a sought-after professional who can thrive in any setting as you become a center for vital knowledge and resources.

Using Emotional Intelligence

Emotional intelligence is required for making and keeping professional connections. Empathy and understanding the feelings of others can help you form solid relationships and create a supporting network that can help you cope during difficult times.

Networking is more than simply a way to develop your business network; it is a powerful instrument for encouraging personal growth and resilience. You may obtain ideas, learn from others, establish a support system, and gain significant mentoring by networking. Furthermore, networking improves your communication skills, emotional intelligence, and collaborative abilities, all of which are important components of resilience. Accept networking as an important part of your professional development, and you will be better prepared to succeed in the face of hardship and uncertainty. As you network with experts from diverse fields, you'll realize that the strength of resilience rests inside yourself and within the supporting network you create along the road.

Creating a Leadership Support System

Leaders' success is determined not just by their qualities and skills but also by the relationships and support they have with others. You need a network of individuals who can provide you with guidance, comments, resources, and support whether you are leading a team, a project, or a change endeavor. But how could such a network emerge among extremely successful leaders? And how did they keep it up over time? Here, we'll look at some practical suggestions and methods they utilized to build and nurture a support network for their leadership path and how you may do the same.

- **Identifying Needs**

The first step in creating a support network is determining what type of assistance is required. Do you require assistance with a specific difficulty or goal? Do you require someone to discuss your thoughts and views with? Do you require motivation and inspiration? Do you require someone to push you and hold you accountable? Depending on your needs, you may wish to search your network for other categories of individuals, such as mentors, coaches, peers, sponsors, allies, or buddies.

- **Seeking and Quality Diversity**

The second stage in developing a support network is to seek out diversity and quality in connections. Diversity entails seeking out individuals with viewpoints, backgrounds, experiences, and abilities that are different from yours. This can assist you in broadening your horizons, learning new skills, and avoiding blind spots. Looking for individuals with high trust, respect, honesty, and reciprocity with you is a sign of quality. This can aid in forming significant and long-lasting bonds that benefit both parties.

- **Reaching Out and Making Connections**

The third phase in developing a support network is reaching out to and engaging with the individuals they wish to include in their network. This needs some bravery and initiative, but it is rewarding and enjoyable. You, too, may begin by identifying individuals you currently know who might assist you and then broaden your network by asking for introductions, attending events, joining clubs, or utilizing social media. When connecting with someone, be upfront about your objective and expectations, and demonstrate genuine attention and admiration for them.

- **Give and Get Value**

Giving and receiving value in their connections is the fourth step leaders take in developing a support network. The value may be defined as everything that contributes to the well-being of another person, such as knowledge, guidance, feedback, acknowledgment, recommendations, or emotional support. Giving value may help create rapport, credibility, and goodwill among network members while also making you feel good. Receiving value may assist you in growing, learning, and achieving your objectives while also making you feel appreciated and encouraged.

- **Maintaining Contact and Following Up**

The fifth stage in developing a support network is to remain in touch with and follow up with network members. This helps preserve and improve their relationships while creating chances for more cooperation and assistance. Keeping in touch can be as simple as sending a message, making a phone call, or setting up a meeting. Following up is as simple as thanking someone, providing an update, or offering assistance. The key to effective communication is to be consistent, courteous, and truthful.

- **Assessing and Modifying**

The sixth phase in developing a support network is to evaluate and change their networks as they progress. Your needs and ambitions, as well as the individuals in your network, may change over time. You could wish to bring in new individuals, eliminate others, or modify the nature of your connections. Evaluating your network may help you determine how effectively it serves you and if there are gaps or possibilities. Shifting your network can help you maximize your support system while respecting others' shifting needs and ambitions.

You'll need a strong support network if you want to make huge changes or achieve large goals. A strong support network makes the difficult times tolerable and the good times more frequent, successful, and pleasurable. Building a strong support network requires time and effort. There are numerous locations to find the proper people, but there are also many sites to locate the wrong ones. However, if you take time and effort to build the correct support network, your results will accelerate.

Leadership Resilience Through Networking

Networking has become an essential component of professional and personal development. Networking is a strong technique that may greatly affect one's professional trajectory and create resilience in the face of adversity. It is more than just swapping business cards and small conversations. As a global leader, I have witnessed firsthand the transforming effect of networking in my personal and professional development path. In this section, I will discuss the significance of networking and how it may help create resilience.

- **Increasing Your Horizons**

Networking allows you to discover new prospects and possibilities. Connecting with people from various backgrounds and sectors lets you gain insights into new viewpoints and ideas. Exposure to various perspectives promotes adaptation and resilience, allowing you to negotiate the uncertainties and complexity of the working world.

- **Learning from Others**

Participating in discussions with professional experts from diverse disciplines gives excellent learning opportunities. You may learn from their achievements and disappointments and be inspired by their perseverance and commitment. Networking helps you seek guidance, gather useful knowledge, and apply it to your journey, giving you the skills, you need to overcome obstacles.

Succession Planning Through Leadership Networking

One of the most strategic measures a leader can take is succession planning. It is an important aspect of good leadership to discover, develop, and retain future leaders inside the business. Succession planning has several advantages, but the process is not without difficulties. There are, however, tried and tested best practices that leaders may use. Organizations that plan ahead of time for leadership transitions will guarantee knowledge transfer, cultural preservation, business continuity, stability, and sustainability. Best practices for ensuring the effectiveness of a succession plan are:

- Identifying talent gaps and developing the next generation of leaders.
- Identifying and mitigating risks associated with leadership departures.
- Securing organizational knowledge.
- Maintaining key aspects of organizational culture.

Furthermore, succession planning allows executives to examine and describe the competencies necessary for successful leadership inside the firm. Succession planning guarantees that possible successors are available inside the company to assume critical responsibilities when existing leaders retire, quit, or leave the business for other reasons. It entails reviewing the organization's present talent, identifying high-potential performers, and providing appropriate support and development opportunities to prepare them for future leadership responsibilities. Succession planning is critical for an organization's continuity, stability, and sustainability. The significance of succession planning cannot be emphasized, and leaders must prepare ahead of time. Those attempting to create an effective succession plan should;

1. **Start the Process Right Away:** Identifying and nurturing potential successors is not always easy. Because of this, leaders must begin succession planning as soon as they assume leadership. By selecting and preparing the ideal successor for each leadership job, organizations will prevent interruptions in business operations, sustain productivity, and ensure a

successful knowledge transfer. Team engagement and retention are also boosted by succession planning. Team members are more likely to be motivated, devoted, and loyal to the business when they perceive a clear route for professional progression and feel that their growth and development are recognized. Succession planning emphasizes continual training and skill-building activities to prepare personnel for future leadership roles, fostering a culture of learning and growth. This, in turn, improves the organization's overall competencies and competitiveness. Finally, succession planning as an early and continuous process contributes to the organization's overall strategy by allowing leaders to proactively address leadership requirements, establish and implement a development plan, and coach team members for the new job. Leaders mitigate the danger of leadership gaps during transition periods by identifying and nurturing future leaders within the business. Organizations may reduce disruption by cultivating and retaining talent early on. Once linked with company objectives, a clear and successful succession plan that is created early improves organizational agility. Leaders give chances for learning and promotion and a plan that helps workers remain engaged and committed by investing in the career development of top performers with high potential. This proactive strategy reduces interruptions, keeps the organization stable, and provides for a smooth succession of duties. Finally, good succession planning ensures the organization has a strong talent pipeline and transferable leadership abilities across many organizational tiers.

2. **Evaluate Internal Talent Against External Skillsets:** Developing a diversified and talented pool of applicants improves the leadership pipeline. Leaders are urged to analyze talent in comparable businesses to ensure that the succession plans developed by the organization are accurate for the organization today and in the future. Leaders may discover internal and external talent with the appropriate skills, knowledge, and experience to effectively lead through specific problems and opportunities that may come in the future by concentrating on establishing a range of competencies. This variety in the talent pool reduces the danger of over-reliance on a single team member and guarantees that a greater range of experiences and competencies are evaluated as part of the succession talent pool, making the company more adaptive and resilient. Leaders who value their team members' growth and development foster an atmosphere that fosters creativity, cooperation, and engagement. Team members notice the organization's efforts to discover what success looks like and to harness internal and external resources to prepare them for success, which improves their commitment. This strategy not only decreases the risk of talent shortages and develops employee loyalty but also builds professional connections and

promotes knowledge-sharing across enterprises. As leaders undertake this endeavor and identify any gaps in leadership qualities that must be addressed to manage risks, the talent development areas that must be prioritized become clear. Leaders will be able to evaluate not just the leadership competencies of leaders in other businesses but also their attention to diversity and recognize and analyze how prior leadership transitions have been carried out. A robust leadership pipeline lessens reliance on individual leaders while fostering a continual development culture. However, selecting successors has obstacles, such as determining the most effective methods of knowledge transfer and determining whether leadership development programs will produce the intended results. Leaders must create a detailed transition plan that outlines the particular duties, objectives, and timetables for each individual participating in the succession process and then assess its efficacy.

Furthermore, developing efficient communication channels and cultivating strong connections between current leaders and successors is critical to the plan's success. When establishing a succession plan, some executives face opposition and hesitancy. This is frequently due to a lack of confidence in training someone else to take over their function, a fear of being undermined, or the chance that their role may be called into doubt. To address this issue, leaders must stress the benefits of succession planning and foster a culture that encourages and rewards leadership development at all levels of the business. Long-term benefits must be communicated, such as higher organizational stability, improved talent retention, additional leadership skills for both the leader and the successor, and increased adaptation to change. Involving existing leaders in succession planning and soliciting their feedback may also help assuage worries and build a feeling of transparency and teamwork. One of the most difficult difficulties for leaders is identifying the ideal successor for their post and finding the time to build and implement the best strategy to guarantee a seamless leadership transition. Leaders who think about these issues and address them early and openly will create trust and be more likely to generate a strong pipeline of competent candidates to enable a smooth leadership transfer when the time comes.

3. **Utilize Mentorship Communication and Transparency:** Effective succession planning requires open and transparent communication. Effective communication keeps possible successors interested and motivated while eliminating organizational ambiguity and conjecture. Giving potential successors comments and direction on their development progress helps them recognize their strengths and areas for growth and provides them with an open communication channel to discuss their careers. Organizations will establish a pipeline of talented leaders and guarantee a seamless transition phase by concentrating on organizational stability, talent development,

and effective communication. Mentorship is essential in the succession planning process since it is an ongoing activity. This is because mentorship allows experienced leaders to pass on their knowledge and skills to prospective successors. Seasoned professionals may convey unique insights, organizational-specific know-how, and vital leadership abilities through a mentor-mentee relationship. This knowledge transfer allows a smooth transition for successors, avoiding disturbance and maintaining organizational continuity. Mentorship also allows for personal and professional development. Mentors act as guides and consultants, providing successors with guidance, encouragement, and critical feedback. This advice assists successors in developing their talents, broadening their viewpoints, and improving their decision-making abilities. It also gives a secure space to address worries and reservations about taking on a more senior job. Organizations guarantee that successors are well-prepared and able to take on leadership challenges by cultivating talent via mentorship, building a culture of continuous improvement, and nurturing a learning culture. Team members will feel supported and appreciated due to this approach and are more likely to be involved in the organization's short- and long-term success. The link formed between mentors and mentees promotes trust, strengthens professional networking, and boosts employee engagement and morale. Organizations may motivate successors to embrace their professional path while enabling a smoother and more successful transfer by actively integrating mentors in the succession planning process. Organizations that promote mentorship programs will enjoy the advantages of a smooth leadership transfer when the time comes.

Succession planning is critical for an organization's top positions to transfer effectively and smoothly. A well-planned succession plan guarantees that the organization can stay stable, continue critical business activities, and maintain long-term success. Organizations may use effective succession planning to identify and nurture high-potential individuals, ensuring they are ready to lead when needed. Organizations may avert big disruptions, decrease risks, and maintain commercial performance by proactively preparing future leaders. There are obvious advantages to succession planning, but there are also obstacles. A company that understands the benefits and accepts the obstacles early on may respond quickly. Organizations that begin the succession planning process early can be more thoughtful and methodical about the process and more comprehensive in developing leadership potential. Leaders must commit time and money to succession planning, which may be regarded as a trade-off for quick benefits, and opposition to change and the unwillingness of present leaders to relinquish their positions can hinder the development of succession planning activities. Given the significance and advantages of succession planning, leaders must prioritize guaranteeing organizational resilience and sustainability. Fostering a culture that promotes and encourages talent development is a call to action for leaders. They should devote time and resources to identifying and developing high-potential team members and giving substantial chances for growth and promotion. Leaders should also develop a disciplined and systematic approach to succession planning, incorporating it into the business's strategic planning process. Leaders may safeguard the future success of their businesses and build a pipeline of competent leaders who are well-prepared to lead the organization forward by actively engaging in succession planning. Leaders may secure their companies' long-term success and sustainability by prioritizing succession planning. Effective succession planning creates a pipeline of qualified leaders ready to manage future problems via strategic talent development, risk reduction, knowledge transfer, and cultural continuity. Leaders who understand the importance of succession planning and use best practices will foster a culture of development, engagement, and resilience in their businesses. Investing in succession planning is a prudent move that sets the tone for a bright and successful future in our ever-changing leadership landscape.

Building Leadership Relationship Trust

I like developing connections as much as I enjoy managing a team. I am fortunate to work with some incredibly wonderful and creative people who make my job simple, but it is not without hard effort and devotion to these connections that we each achieve our collective goals. Here are the top five tactics highly successful leaders use to develop mutually beneficial and strategic connections that help them WIN as a TEAM.

Making People a Priority for Their Goals and Achievement

One of the methods that helped them succeed was knowing critical information about their team members. What college did they attend? What organizations or philanthropies do they belong to? Alternatively, what leaders do they find inspiring? The most crucial component in developing a relationship with your staff is learning these personal details about them. When people realize that you have invested time in learning about them without constantly having to ask them, they will be more open to forming a connection with you.

Genuine Communication Style

Sheryl Sandberg, Facebook's COO, discusses the significance of communication in advancing one's career and business partnerships. Instead of declaring views as facts, she suggests stating beliefs and the facts supporting them and encouraging others to do the same to foster greater information exchange. She also urges everyone to accept full responsibility for their acts and to personalize them, adding that this ownership is an important building block at all phases of one's career.

It is critical not just to one's career but also to the careers of others you influence. Maintaining your authenticity will encourage those around you to be more open to your recommendations since they will be more valuable because they come from a place of truth.

Developing Consistent Value

One sure-fire method effective leaders use to create constant value is empowering team members. Too frequently, leaders act as "fixers," assuming the role of Super-Hero and attempting to "save the day" when their teams present them with difficulty. When, in fact, this devalues their connections with their teams. Giving people tools to solve problems while holding them accountable can build a more open and collaborative atmosphere. When you encourage your team members' freedom, you may better acknowledge their work, making every contact more worthwhile.

Facetime is more valuable than "FaceTime."

Virtual meetings may appear to be the most convenient and straightforward alternative in today's environment. However, strong leaders influence and potentially modify their habits, and they do so in person. We can only create trust through nonverbal communication cues by giving and receiving. Not everyone you lead will always like you, but they must be able to trust you to be persuaded enough to change.

Being Themselves

It reminds me every day that while there are many individuals I respect, attempt to learn from, or copy, the greatest gift I can offer to my team and myself is simply being myself. This is one of the tactics great leaders use to establish team relationships. What you can offer to the table as an individual is unique to you. So, learn to establish and use your unique selling points. Your team and business will be pleased.

Leadership success is difficult because it is based nearly entirely on others' opinions of leaders and their continuous, reciprocal connection rather than merely on leaders' abilities and qualities. There is very little a leader can accomplish and succeed without the support of others in the company, a truth that frequently catches us off guard when it hurts the most. There is a high likelihood of success in leadership if one is rigorous about understanding the nature of the team, selecting and creating relationships with the right individuals, and taking adequate care to nourish and maintain those relationships.

In the following chapter, I will describe how great leaders balance ambition and ethical concerns, making judgments that are consistent with their ideals and how you might do the same.

Chapter 6

Balancing Ambition and Ethics

"The challenge of leadership is to be strong but not rude; be kind, but not weak; be bold, but not a bully; be thoughtful, but not lazy; be humble, but not timid; be proud, but not arrogant; have humor, but without folly." – Jim Rohn

A mbition knows no limits. It fires our dreams, motivates us to strive for perfection, and propels us forward. It is the spark that lights the fire within us, encouraging us to make a positive difference in the world. However, beyond its inspirational surface is a dark side that can potentially convert ambition into a destructive force. When ambition meets a dogged desire for power, even the most well-meaning individuals can become potential agents of destruction.

Ambition, like a double-edged blade, has a lethal side that is frequently veiled. When driven purely by a desire for power and recognition, we become ignorant of the ethical boundaries we should never cross. It fosters a culture of distrust, competitiveness, and deception, all of which impair cooperation and shared accomplishment. When pursuing lofty objectives, it is critical to recognize the importance of basic concepts and values in directing ethical ambitions. They give clear direction and counsel to help you navigate the path to success.

Foundations of Ethical Leadership

Trust and prosperity are built on ethical leadership. It includes the beliefs and behaviors that define a company's culture and influence relationships with employees and stakeholders. Organizations that embrace ethical leadership may provide the groundwork for long-term growth and profitability. Ethical leadership cultivates a culture of trust and credibility, which boosts team engagement, productivity, and overall performance. Integrity, fairness, honesty, and accountability are priorities for ethical leaders. They set a good example for their teams by regularly making moral judgments and acting clearly.

It is impossible to overestimate the importance of ethical leadership in establishing trust and confidence. Leaders acquire their team members' and stakeholders' confidence and respect when they display ethical behavior and continuously operate with integrity. Ethical leaders behave transparently, communicate honestly, and accept responsibility for their judgments. This degree of transparency and accountability fosters confidence and credibility inside and outside the organization.

Making decisions based on principles is an important part of ethical leadership. Ethical leaders assure fairness, justice, and ethical behavior by making moral judgments, thus increasing trust and credibility. Ethical leaders examine the possible influence of their actions on diverse stakeholders, considering ethical concerns and long-term implications. They seek to make decisions consistent with their and the organization's ideals.

Ethical leadership also improves team engagement and productivity. Team members feel confident and encouraged to offer their best effort when they see their leaders constantly making ethical judgments and acting with integrity. Ethical leaders foster a welcoming and inclusive workplace where team members feel appreciated and respected. This creates a sense of psychological safety among followers and allows them to express their thoughts, discuss their ideas, and work productively. Team members are more engaged, dedicated, and productive when they trust their leaders and believe in the organization's ethics.

Furthermore, ethical leadership sets the tone for the organization's broader ethical atmosphere. Followers or team members are more likely to embrace and reflect these beliefs in their behavior when leaders prioritize ethics and constantly enforce ethical standards. Ethical leadership fosters an environment of integrity in which people feel encouraged to behave morally, even in difficult situations. This common commitment to ethical behavior fosters a healthy work environment, strengthens connections, and improves the organization's overall reputation.

Furthermore, ethical leadership is necessary for establishing trust and confidence. Ethical leaders make ethical judgments, behave with integrity, and prioritize stakeholders' well-being. Beyond trust and credibility, ethical leadership has a favorable influence on team engagement and productivity. Organizations may build an ethical environment to foster a culture of honesty, fairness, and responsibility, leading to long-term success and sustainable connections with team members and stakeholders.

Balancing Personal Ambition and Team Collaboration

Effective leadership is not just wielding power and control but also nurturing and elevating people who look to you for guidance. It is the delicate balance between personal desire and teamwork. Striking a balance between these two seemingly conflicting forces is critical for effective leadership that develops cooperation, stimulates organizational growth, and creates a healthy work environment. Personal ambition is the intrinsic drive to achieve greatness, ascend the leadership ladder, and greatly affect one's surroundings. Ambitious leaders frequently establish lofty goals for themselves, have a strong desire to succeed, and are prepared to take calculated risks to attain their goals.

While ambition may inspire energy and invention, it can lead to self-centeredness, disrespect for others, and a competitive spirit. All of these characteristics ultimately work against collaboration. Self-awareness is the first step in becoming an effective and successful leader who balances personal ambition with collaboration. Understanding one's goals, strengths, shortcomings, and how these impact team dynamics is critical.

Reflect on your behaviors, decisions, and reasons regularly. Identifying instances where personal desire may have taken precedence over teamwork will allow you to make purposeful adjustments.

Leaders and aspiring leaders should create a compelling vision that goes beyond their personal goals. A shared purpose corresponding to the firm's values may unite the team and develop a collective commitment to a common goal. Your team will be more driven to participate and collaborate if they sense that you emphasize the greater good over individual achievement. Effective leaders also recognize that they cannot do everything on their own. Delegating tasks to team members lighten the strain and allows them to take ownership of their work. This helps team members improve their skills and confidence, eventually strengthening their capabilities. However, keep in mind that not every work needs your particular attention. The finest leaders are those who fit in as another colleague inside the group. You wouldn't be able to determine who the team's leader is from the outside.

Delegate tasks corresponding to team members' areas of expertise and interests, allowing them to take ownership and participate successfully.

While individual desire may drive individual ambitions, it is critical to establish objectives that promote teamwork and team accomplishment. You may foster a sense of togetherness and create an environment where everyone is committed to each other's success by including the team in goal-setting and stressing shared successes. Furthermore, praise individual accomplishments, milestones, and efforts to develop an appreciation culture. Recognizing extraordinary accomplishments in public enhances team spirit and inspires others to succeed.

The Dangers of Unethical Ambition

In today's environment, success is frequently chased with zeal. Ambitious CEOs sometimes attempt to ascend the corporate ladder at the expense of others. However, the saying "the wrong always comes to the one who did" is accurate, reminding us that unethical behavior and disrespect for the well-being of others inevitably lead to personal and professional failure. In this text portion, I will discuss the repercussions of unethical objectives and why adopting ethical behavior and truth is critical.

The Cost of Unethical Success

While success can be rewarding in the short term, it has serious ramifications when obtained in dishonest or unethical ways. Engaging in actions that injure or exploit others may offer short-term rewards, but the long-term consequences outweigh any short-term gains. Ethical breaches weaken trust, harm relationships, and tarnish reputations, stifling growth and advancement.

The Effects of Unethical Behavior

Unethical behavior not only has an immediate impact on the leader engaged, but it also has larger ramifications for the business as a whole. When one person's success is based on the misfortunes of others, a poisonous work atmosphere is created. Morale among team members diminishes, resulting in lower production and a greater turnover rate. Furthermore, firms with a reputation for unethical conduct suffer long-term brand harm and significant legal implications, limiting their profitability.

The Power of Truth

Truth has an intrinsic robustness that cannot be overlooked. No matter how hard one tries to hide or twist facts, the truth eventually comes to light. In the workplace and among coworkers, honesty and integrity are highly respected. Individuals who embrace these ideals create an environment that fosters open communication, cooperation, and trust.

Furthermore, honesty fosters trust, laying the groundwork for professional connections and boosting one's reputation.

Embracing Ethical Behavior

Organizations must highlight the value of integrity and fair play to foster an ethical culture. Encourage open communication and provide ethical decision-making training to team members to help them negotiate challenging circumstances with honesty and openness. Rewarding and recognizing ethical conduct can encourage people to make principled decisions, establishing a healthy and respected working atmosphere.

Setting a Good Example

Organizational leaders have a critical role in setting the tone for ethical behavior. They motivate their colleagues to follow suit by exemplifying integrity and following ethical standards in their actions and judgments. Effective leaders recognize that achieving success by ethical methods is sustainable and advantageous to the organization's long-term growth. Their dedication to the truth fosters a culture of justice, collaboration, and respect.

While the desire for success is normal, it is critical to remember that genuine success is founded on ethical foundations. The adage "the wrong always comes back to the one who did" emphasizes the repercussions of ignoring the well-being of others for personal benefit. Ethical behavior is essential for effective leadership because the truth always triumphs. Organizations and leaders may thrive in a climate that values honesty, integrity, and justice, knowing their accomplishments are well-deserved.

Balancing Ambition with Mental and Physical Health

As leaders try to reach our objectives and become the greatest versions of ourselves, it's easy to overlook the necessity of maintaining our mental and physical health. In the quest for achievement, we frequently push ourselves to the edge, forsaking sleep, proper food, and exercise. Neglecting our well-being, on the other hand, can have a negative impact on our performance, productivity, and overall enjoyment. In this section, I will explain the notion of self-care and how to reconcile ambition with mental and physical health.

- **The Value of Self-Care**

Self-care is actively maintaining and enhancing one's health and well-being. It entails making deliberate decisions to prioritize our mental, emotional, and physical needs. Self-care may appear to be a luxury or a selfish act, yet it is essential for sustaining good health and functioning. We become more vulnerable to stress, burnout, sickness, and other negative outcomes when we disregard our well-being.

- **Recognize Burnout Symptoms**

Burnout is a condition characterized by physical, emotional, and mental depletion as a result of extended stress. It's typical for high-achievers who push themselves too hard and ignore their self-care. Chronic exhaustion, sleeplessness, irritability, anxiety, sadness, and decreased productivity are all symptoms of burnout. If you suffer any of these symptoms, you must step back and prioritize your health.

- **Incorporate Self-Care Practices into Your Daily Routine**

Everyone defines self-care differently, but some typical practices include getting adequate sleep, eating a balanced diet, exercising regularly, practicing mindfulness, and setting boundaries. It is critical to prioritize self-care and include it in your daily routine. You may, for example, make time for exercise or meditation, emphasize healthy food preparation, or limit work hours and social responsibilities.

- **Strive for a Healthy Balance of Ambition and Self-Care**

Pursuing your objectives while simultaneously prioritizing your emotional and physical wellness is feasible. Self-care may improve your performance and productivity by increasing your attention, creativity, and energy levels. Setting realistic objectives corresponding to your beliefs and skills is one approach to balancing ambition and self-care. When faced with setbacks or disappointments, taking breaks and exercising self-compassion is critical.

- **Seek Expert Help**

If you are suffering from extreme stress, burnout, or mental health difficulties, you must get expert assistance. Therapy, counseling, or medical care may be included. Don't be afraid to seek help when you need it since addressing your mental and physical health is critical for long-term success.

Self-care is critical for balancing ambition and mental and physical wellness. Understanding self-care's value, recognizing burnout symptoms, including self-care activities in your daily routine, balancing ambition with self-care, and getting professional help are all critical steps toward attaining optimal well-being and leadership success.

So far in this chapter, we can see that mastering the delicate balance of ambition and ethics in leadership needs ongoing self-reflection, adherence to ethical standards, and a willingness to favor long-term repercussions above short-term advantages. We can successfully navigate ethical boundaries and build sustainable and successful leadership that thrives in an ever-changing world by recognizing ethical quandaries, cultivating values-based leadership, fostering transparency and accountability, balancing short-term ambitions, and seeking guidance.

In the next chapter, we will analyze the secrets of the world's famous leaders, how they achieved such greatness, and how you might imitate and follow their footsteps.

Let's get started!

Chapter 7

Life And Success Secrets of Highly Successful Leaders

"The secret of success is to do the common things uncommonly well." – John D. Rockefeller

W hat qualities distinguish an effective leader? Some define it by the bottom line, while others measure it by organizational culture, connection, and purpose. For the greatest results, a combination of all of these and more. As I often say, matching the proper leadership style to the right situation is essential. Leaders need to link their approach to what is needed to maximize performance and be flexible enough to modify their approach when circumstances change.

Inspiring leaders are wonderful people with strong character traits and values such as perspective, generosity, and inclusivity. What leaders exude as individuals is just as significant as what they say and do." So, what is it about CEOs like Elon Musk, Bill Gates, and Mary Barra that has led to their success? These CEOs, you see, have at least two major things in common. First, they aim for the moon (or, in Musk's case, Mars). They have lofty, bold, and time-bound goals. They may not transmit the 'how,' but they do convey the direction. They understand that setting clear, provocative, and strong directions is one of everyone in power's most crucial leadership jobs. Second, they instill a leadership culture throughout their organizations. They understand that they cannot address the most difficult problems alone and that their job is to foster a culture of creativity, experimentation, and disruption."

So, how have these characteristics shown themselves throughout history? From inexpensive vehicles to transporting humans to space, technology is altering the globe. We'll delve into the success stories and personal traits of some of the most inspiring businessmen of the last century and a half.

Henry Ford

Henry Ford, the founder of Ford Motor Company, was born on July 30, 1863, in Springwells Township, Wayne County, Michigan, to Mary Litogot and William Ford. Of the six children—four boys and two girls—he was the eldest.

His father was an immigrant to America in 1847, originally from County Cork, Ireland, and he farmed in Wayne County.

Young Henry Ford was fascinated with mechanics. By the age of 12, he spent most of his free time in a tiny machine shop he had built. At the age of 15, he built his first steam engine there.

Later, he worked as a machinist's apprentice at James F. Flower and Brothers shops and the Detroit Dry Dock Company in Detroit. After finishing his apprenticeship in 1882, he spent a year in southern Michigan putting up and servicing Westinghouse steam engines. In July 1891, he started working as an engineer for the Detroit-based Edison Illuminating Company. In 1893, on November 6, he became the head engineer. Henry Ford would consider Thomas Edison to be a lifelong mentor and friend.

Henry married Clara Jane Bryant of Greenfield, Michigan, the daughter of Martha (Bench) and Melvin Bryant, a Wayne County farmer, on April 11, 1888. Clara died on September 29, 1950, at the age of 84. On November 6, 1893, Edsel Bryant Ford, their only child, was born. Henry Ford's interest in internal combustion engines led him to create a simple one-cylinder gasoline model in the winter of 1893, marking the beginning of his career as an automobile maker. The first Ford engine flickered to life on a wooden table in the kitchen of the Ford house at 58 Bagley Avenue in Detroit. His first vehicle, just a frame mounted with four bicycle wheels, was powered by a later version of that engine. In June 1896, Ford manufactured its first car, the Quadricycle.

He left the Edison Illuminating Company in 1899 and joined up with associates to found the Detroit Automobile Company, which failed within around 18 months. Meanwhile, Henry Ford created and manufactured several racing automobiles. On October 10, 1901, he won the Sweepstakes by defeating Alexander Winton on a track in Grosse Pointe, Michigan. One month later, Henry Ford established his second vehicle company, the Henry Ford Company. In early 1902, he left the company that would become the Cadillac Motor Car Company. In 1904, on the winter ice of Lake St. Clair, he set a world record for the mile in another of his racing vehicles, the 999, covering the distance in 39.4 seconds.

On June 16, 1903, Henry Ford and 12 other investors contributed $28,000 to establish the Ford Motor Company. The first car sold by the firm was on July 15, 1903. Henry controlled 25.5% of the new company's equity. He was appointed president and key owner in 1906. In 1919, Henry, Clara, and Edsel Ford paid $105,820,894 to buy out all minority shares and became the sole proprietors of the company. Edsel, who replaced his father as president in 1919, held the role until he died in 1943 when Henry Ford reclaimed it.

When he resigned from the presidency for the second time in September 1945, Henry Ford urged his grandson, Henry Ford II, to be elected. His recommendation was approved by the board of directors.

Henry Ford was honored for his services to the automobile industry at the Automobile Golden Jubilee in 1946. In July that year, 50,000 people applauded him at a massive 83rd birthday party in Dearborn. Later that year, the American Petroleum Institute gave him its first Gold Medal yearly award for distinguished contributions to humanity's welfare. In 1965, the United States government honored him with a postage stamp showing his portrait with a Model T as part of their Prominent Americans series. Fortune Magazine selected Henry Ford as the Businessman of the Century in 1999.

You may want to be as successful as, if not more successful than, Henry Ford, whose accomplishments impressed and inspired immense fulfilment. But ask yourself, "What factors contributed to Henry Ford's success as a leader and businessman?" "How did he go from being the son of a farmer to becoming a well-known inventor?"

Here are six vital tips that helped Henry Ford become a great, successful entrepreneur and leader, and these six secrets may also assist you.

Secrets of Henry Ford's Success

- **Tip 1: Adoption of Cutting-Edge Technology**

You've probably heard or read that Henry Ford invented the assembly line. He has utilized and expanded on this concept, but it does not belong to him as an original work.

What factors contributed to Henry Ford's success as an entrepreneur, if not the manufacturing line? In reality, he is the father of mass-production automobile manufacturing. The assembly line was placed into production due to Henry Ford's goal to make an automobile affordable to ordinary Americans.

How did he develop the concept of using an assembly line in mechanical engineering? Ford visited the mill in the early twentieth century and witnessed how the moving animal corpses dropped under the blades of the dividers. He upgraded his factories' technology by adding belts to the conveyor.

- **Tip 2: Good Working Circumstances**

Caring for team members was one of Henry Ford's most important ideals. He was the one who changed the working day from 10 to eight hours. As a result, he offered a five-dollar-per-day minimum salary, which was about double the national average wage, and a 40-hour workday.

What else contributed to Henry Ford's entrepreneurial success? He stated that he required the labor force and was experiencing staff churn. He could fully staff his plants thanks to a significant rise in pay. Furthermore, he won on job quality because of personnel who had worked at the company for over a year. These individuals generated more products of higher quality than novices.

Henry Ford was the first to provide annual bonuses to managers and regular employees, with the payouts always contingent on the company's results. Was it a significant factor in Henry Ford's success as an entrepreneur? Absolutely, because he also provided discounts and payment plans to his employees when they purchased automobiles. His desire to create the greatest advertisement possible to attract new clients was justified.

He also determined that each employee should be accountable for his or her case rather than doing everything all at once. It enables a worker to complete an assignment more effectively since he is not distracted by another procedure.

- **Tip 3: Making People Pay Democratic Prices.**

Henry Ford was the first to make the automobile a mass industrial development item. His people's vehicle (Ford-T) manufacture began in 1908. That was a game changer in terms of mass manufacturing and cost savings. At that period, the typical price of an automobile ranged from $1000 to $5000. Following Ford's entry into the worldwide market, vehicle costs decreased precipitously. He began selling his Ford-T for $850, but by 1916, the price had fallen to $360. That is the other factor contributing to Henry Ford's success as an entrepreneur.

Many people are familiar with Henry Ford's famous quip about black vehicles. Actually, that was the only way to reduce car prices. The rationale was not because of aesthetics but because self-colored painting reduced production costs. Every day, Ford looked for ways to cut expenses by even a penny without losing quality.

- **Tip 4: Having Faith**

According to Henry Ford, people who are terrified of failure restrict their options. Did you ever consider what contributed to Henry Ford's success as an entrepreneur? If a genius inventor was scared to take chances and didn't trust in himself, the world would never hear about him.

Banks declined him loans on many occasions at the start of his career. Many ideas and a shortage of funds drove him to learn how to bargain. Henry Ford persuaded investors to grant him 86 thousand dollars (approximately $2.6 million now) because of his tenacity and conviction in himself. It seemed incredible that an unknown inventor could get significant businesspeople to invest in his ideas.

Initially, Henry's innovations were not in high demand. He traveled around the city in his automobile to capture the attention of possible investors and consumers. It was the identical car that Ford had built in his garage without the assistance of anybody else. The people mocked Henry Ford and labeled him as obsessive. Was this one of the factors that contributed to Henry Ford's success as an entrepreneur? Without a doubt, he refused to give up and was not scared to be ridiculed.

Ford competed in car racing and won the United States championship. The inventor's primary goal was to promote the automobile and display its nobility. It resulted in an effective marketing effort.

- **Tip 5: Putting Service Before Profit.**

Furthermore, Ford considered that profit could not be the company's primary purpose. It should be the prize for meticulous service and a genuine desire to assist everyone. He believes money is just a tool that can be used to better situations and advance their growth.

It does not imply that the manufacturing is only based on purchasing low and selling high. It was the procedure of purchasing resources fairly with the minimum feasible monetary addition and ready-for-sale product for Henry Ford. Roguery and speculation are the primary opponents of doing business, as they merely slow things down. In his opinion, a good businessman is a wise and seasoned mind.

- **Tip 6: Fight the Good Fight for Success**

Do you want to know the final cause behind Henry Ford's entrepreneurial success? Ford also avoided fierce rivalry because he thought trying to steal another person's business was illegal. He claimed that any matter must be governed by logic, not force. As a result, the time spent researching competitors is better spent on conducting business.

The same is true for hiring employees at his plant. Henry Ford only allowed healthy competition, so he employed more productive workers. The firm's productivity grew by 51% due to this choice. Furthermore, absenteeism was cut in half, and absence for good reasons was substantially reduced. Ford's profits climbed from $30 million to $60 million in two years as a result of his new business perspective.

Henry Ford's life and accomplishments are inspiring and serve as a model for leaders and aspiring leaders to emulate.

Steve Jobs

One name stands out as a light of genius in technology and innovation: Steve Jobs. Steve Jobs, the co-founder of Apple Inc., had a distinctive influence on the technology sector and how we live our lives today. His journey from humble origins to tech legend is one of perseverance, invention, and unflinching vision. Steve Jobs was born on the 24th of February, 1955, in San Francisco. Paul and Clara Jobs adopted him and fostered his early interest in electronics. Jobs' interest in technology drove him to experiment with devices in his garage, which would eventually become the cradle of Apple. Steve Jobs founded Apple Computer, Inc. with his buddy Steve Wozniak in 1976. They aimed to make user-friendly computers that anybody, not just IT specialists, could use. The introduction of the Apple I and Apple II computers signaled the start of a revolution in personal computing. Steve was still in high school, and Wozniak was in college, but the two shared interests in electronics, technology, and tinkering.

Steve attended college in Oregon after graduating high school but immediately became bored and quit. Jobs saw college as pointless, a waste of his parents' money, and unrelated to his goals. As a result, he returned to live with his parents and got work at videogame manufacturer Atari. However, Jobs' stay would be brief, as he would shortly journey to India to pursue enlightenment.

Jobs would return to the United States after seven months overseas. When he returned, he finally regained work with Atari, and shortly after, he and Wozniak began their technological adventures in his parents' garage.

They began by creating and selling circuit boards to tech businesses and computer tinkerers like him and Wozniak. But then they had the bright notion to develop the personal computer. So, they sold a handful of their valuables to fund their endeavor and created their company, Apple, and their first product, the Apple I.

With Steve Jobs as the company's major visionary and creator, he reached for the stars, relying primarily on his individually crafted goal to "change the world through technology."

Their first product did have some early success, as they sold around 88% of the 200 units made. However, after obtaining a few more investors and releasing a newly upgraded computer, the Apple II, they decommissioned their initial product (just a circuit board).

Making a few minor improvements, such as incorporating a monitor and keyboard inside the circuit board as a unit, enabled them to launch this new device to stratospheric heights of success. The Apple II would become one of the world's most successful and first mass-produced personal computers.

From then on, Steve Jobs and Wozniak's company would take off. After the Apple II, they released several devices to compete with IBM for supremacy in the personal computer industry.

Apple, as well as Steve Jobs' money, would soar to dizzying heights. Jobs' net wealth had risen to $250 million two years later from $1 million in 1978. The corporation was also worth more than a billion dollars in the market.

Unfortunately for Steve Jobs, the celebration did not endure long. When IBM introduced the PC, the company's mission shifted from innovation to market share defense. By 1985, Steve Jobs was clashing with the newly appointed CEO about the company's future direction and how to stay relevant.

Their conflicts were so vehement that Jobs was finally forced out of his firm. Apple's CEO, Steve Jobs, resigned. He didn't, however, let being forced out of his firm bring him down. Instead, he picked himself up and returned to doing what he does best: producing. Jobs would later found another computer business, suitably named NeXT Inc.

Jobs was quite serious about starting a new chapter in his life. He aggressively sought out investors for the next stage of his life and successfully assembled a firm and several items that would become highly sought after and perform well in the marketplace.

He would also make significant investments in the animation firm that would ultimately be known as Disney's Pixar. Indeed, Jobs remained true to his fundamental objective of "changing the world through technology."

After only a few years, NeXT would become so successful that Apple would attempt to acquire them. And they purchased it. Following this acquisition in 1997, Steve Jobs returned to Apple as an advisor. But, soon after his return, he would reclaim the top leadership position, resuming the helm as CEO. After taking back control of Apple, Jobs played a pivotal role in revitalizing the company. For years, the firm had been losing money under the previous CEO. Apple has been losing billions of dollars in market share yearly for several years.

When Jobs returned to his former position, he accomplished the unthinkable: he virtually single-handedly reversed the company's path.

Steve Jobs' strategy differed greatly from those of those before him, whom he finally replaced. Jobs introduced several unique items, beginning with the iMac, a markedly different machine in that it was now Windows-compatible.

He then dramatically reorganized Apple, raising R&D spending considerably and altering Apple's branding into something trendy and current. Jobs' method appeared to purposefully do things differently than the rest — breaking the mold for the technology business.

Following the iMac, Jobs steered Apple into becoming a digital convergence firm, releasing the iPod, iTunes, Apple TV, and the iPhone. Steve Jobs helped Apple achieve a net income of $3.49 billion and a market value of $173 billion by the end of 2007. But, by the time Jobs died in October 2011, Apple's market valuation had risen to approximately $300 billion.

Jobs' basic strategy has drastically changed since his early Apple II days. His first objective when he founded Apple was to "change the world through technology," he accomplished this by being eager to innovate and create products that focused on even the smallest aspects.

Steve Jobs stayed true to his initial concept regardless of the firm he worked with. As a result, he was able to build for customers something that other firms are still attempting to replicate: simple-to-use personal technological gadgets with exceptional design and craftsmanship.

Secrets of Steve Jobs' Success

When people aspire to be more successful, they frequently become less critical.

It's time to rediscover the true meaning of success. Money can be a factor but cannot be the primary motivator. You cannot achieve success if you are a horrible guy. That's simply how things operate.

Consider a truly successful individual in several respects. As an example, consider Steve Jobs. He had a lot of ideas. He understood when and how to take chances. He didn't let billions blind him to his fundamental ideals.

This individual contributed much to the world. We might at least try to learn from his example. I'll tell you five exclusive secrets to help you succeed like Steve Jobs did.

- **Tip 1: Imagine the Future**

Successful individuals anticipate where events will take them. Then, they steer the ship in that direction.

Steve Jobs admired Wayne Gretzky's remark, "I skate to where the puck is going to be, not where it has been." This is an excellent mantra to live by if you want to be successful. Jobs was gifted at foreseeing and creating future trends. The iPhone changed the way we live. This mentality applies to any career. For example, keep up with new approaches if you are a physiotherapist, and do your best to advance them. Aim for advancement so that you do not stagnate.

- **Tip 2: Consider the Opinions of Others**

Steve Jobs was successful because he constantly considered the user's perspective. He wanted to know the ideal user experience, and he continued attempting to provide it. One of his success secrets was his dedication to excellence. Whatever you do, always attempt to make others pleased with your actions. Consider how your actions may affect their life. Every employment involves giving items or services to others. Because you are connected to people, you should do everything possible to improve their experience.

- **Tip 3: Concentrate on the Positive**

When Nike CEO Mark Parker contacted Steve Jobs for business counsel in 2006, Jobs said, "Nike makes some of the best products in the world." Products that you desire. But you also produce a lot of garbage. Simply get rid of the bad and concentrate on the positive."

Right on target, right? Find and exaggerate the good parts of your job. Identify and overcome the disadvantages. If you're seeking a sure-fire formula for success, this is it.

- **Tip 4: Do Something You Enjoy**

Steve Jobs, as everyone knows, dropped out of college. He was intelligent enough to study without any difficulty. It wasn't a lack of dedication. He recognized he wasn't meant to waste his time on something he didn't care about.

He began taking classes that piqued his interest, but he soon dropped out of college because he thought he was squandering his parents' money.

No, I'm not suggesting you drop out of college.

The lesson here is that if something doesn't seem right or align with your future goals, don't waste time with it.

If you're unhappy with your employment, consider alternative possibilities. Why don't you simply do it if you genuinely want to do something different with your life?

- **Tip 5: Learn from Past Mistakes**

A recommendation like "don't allow yourself to fail" has no place in a realistic success handbook. Nobody succeeds. It's just the way humans are. Steve Jobs was dismissed from Apple, his firm, in 1984.

In a speech to Stanford graduates in 2005, he highlighted how his failure helped him grow: "I didn't see it at the time, but getting fired from Apple turned out to be the best thing that could have ever happened to me." The burden of achievement was replaced by the lightness of being a beginning once more, less certain about things. It allowed me to enter one of my most creative times."

Failure is not the end of the world. Consider it a new beginning in your life. What are your plans after that?

It is not always simple to achieve success. It nearly never comes easily. We have a lot to learn, but thankfully, great leaders like Steve Jobs can teach us the most important things.

Despite being considered rigorous, Jobs' leadership style instilled loyalty and performance in his workforce. He was known for pushing the limits of creativity and expecting the best of himself and those around him. His journey from youthful, tech-savvy dreamer to Apple Inc. co-founder is a monument to the power of creativity, tenacity, and a never-ending quest for greatness. His influence on the technology sector and the globe at large is incalculable. Jobs' tale has inspired generations of entrepreneurs and inventors to "think differently."

Madam C.J. Walker

On December 23, 1867, Madam C.J. Walker was born. Owen and Minerva, her parents, were Louisiana sharecroppers who were born into slavery. Sarah, their sixth child, was the first freeborn child in her family following the Emancipation Proclamation. Her childhood was filled with adversity. She was orphaned at seven, married at fourteen (to Moses McWilliams, with whom she had a daughter, A'Lelia, in 1885), and died as a widow at the age of twenty.

Walker moved to St. Louis with her 2-year-old daughter A'Lelia, where she continued to attend night classes and worked as a laundress. She performed in the St. Paul African Methodist Episcopal Church choir and got involved with the National Association of Colored Women. She first met Charles J. Walker in St. Louis, the man who would become her second husband and inspire the name of her future empire.

Walker was motivated to produce haircare products for Black women after experiencing hair loss due to a scalp disease. She devised a solution that will fundamentally transform the Black hair care market.

Walker's approach, dubbed the "Walker system," included scalp prep, moisturizers, and iron combs. Her handmade pomade was a huge hit. While there were other products for Black hair on the market (mostly made by white corporations), she distinguished hers by highlighting its focus on the health of the women who would use it. She offered her handcrafted items to Black women directly, utilizing a personal approach that earned her a devoted clientele. She hired a slew of saleswomen to peddle the product, whom she dubbed "beauty culturalists."

Walker got to Denver, Colorado, with only $1.05 in her pocket in 1905. Her goods, such as Wonderful Hair Grower, Glossine, and Vegetable Shampoo, began to attract a dedicated following, and her fortunes began to change. Charles J. Walker went to Denver in 1906, and they married shortly after that. Her spouse initially assisted her with marketing, advertising, and mail orders, but they became estranged and divorced as the business progressed.

Walker named a beauty school and factory after her daughter in Pittsburgh, Pennsylvania, in 1908. She relocated her corporate headquarters to Indianapolis in 1910, a city with train connections for distribution and many African American clients. She gave A'Lelia command of the Pittsburgh branch. By the time she died, Madame C.J.

Walker Company had employed about 40,000 individuals, mostly Black women who marketed Walker's wares.

Walker became one of the most well-known African Americans, and the Black press loved him. Her economic success enabled her to live in residences far removed from the one she had grown up in; when her daughter acquired her Manhattan townhouse in the 1920s, it was transformed into a Harlem Renaissance salon. Vertner Tandy, a Black architect, designed Walker's country home, Villa Lewaro, in Irvington-on-Hudson.

Walker's entrepreneurial prominence was only rivaled by her philanthropic renown. She formed employee groups, encouraging them to give back to their communities and rewarded them with incentives when they did so. She pushed female talent at a period when positions for Black women were few, even mandating in her company's charter that only a woman may serve as president. She generously gave to educational causes and Black charities, sponsoring Tuskegee Institute scholarships for women and giving to the NAACP, the Black YMCA, and hundreds of other organizations that helped shape Black history.

Madam Walker died of hypertension on May 25, 1919, at the age of 51, at her rural house in Irvington-on-Hudson. Her ideas for the Walker Building in Indianapolis were carried out after her death and finished in 1927. She is known today as a trailblazing Black female businesswoman who influenced many with her financial independence, business skills, and generosity.

Secrets of Madam C.J. Walker's Success

Madam C.J. Walker's life and success story revealed a constantly imaginative and accomplished businesswoman and leader credited with being the first African American self-made millionaire. She made money selling handcrafted hair and hygiene products to Black women and is still well-known in the Black community for her humanitarian endeavors. Is there a formula for this woman's success? Yes! There most certainly is. I'll guide you through some insider secrets that helped her become one of the world's most successful entrepreneurs and leaders.

- **Tip 1: Stay Ahead of the Curve**

In 1913, women made up less than 10% of licensed drivers. Madam Walker had three cars: a Ford Model T, a Waverly Electric, and a seven-passenger luxury Cole Touring Car. She liked her Waverly for afternoon outings to the movies. That year, she transported Cole and her chauffeur on a foreign sales tour to Cuba, Haiti, Jamaica, Panama, and Costa Rica.

Today, we take our favorite retailers' hundreds of hair care products for granted. However, when Walker began her firm more than a century ago, the cosmetics industry was in its infancy. She pioneered what is now a multi-billion-dollar multinational beauty and personal care products market, with contemporaries such as Helena Rubinstein and Elizabeth Arden.

- **Tip 2: Allow Your Light to Shine**

Madam Walker recognized the value of advertisement. She aggressively featured her picture on her products to attract her main clientele of African-American women at a period when the dominant standard of

110

beauty was European hair texture and facial characteristics. She promoted heavily in black publications, using testimonial endorsements and "before and after" images that are still successful today. Her wares were well-known and widely disseminated throughout the United States and the Caribbean long before radio, television, the Internet, and social media.

- **Tip 3: Enabling Others**

During the early 1900s, when most black women were barred from working outside the home or on farms, Madam Walker provided a road to financial independence and less struggle. Her salespeople bragged about earning money to educate their children, buy real estate, and give to charitable organizations at her yearly conferences. A woman said in an email, "You made it possible for me to earn more money in a week than I could in a month working in someone else's kitchen."

Except for her attorney and business manager, Freeman B. Ransom, most of Walker's senior executives were women, including her manufacturing manager, national sales manager, and bookkeeper.

- **Tip 4: Be Brave and Courageous**

Madam Walker commissioned Vertner Woodson Tandy, one of New York State's first licensed black architects, to create her Hudson River-view house in Irvington, New York. In August 1918, she officially inaugurated the mansion with a convention of civil rights leaders and performances by the greatest black artists of the day. Following her mother's death in 1919, her daughter carried on the tradition of significant parties, welcoming Liberia's president for a magnificent,

111

fireworks-filled Fourth of July weekend in 1921. It is a National Historic Landmark and was declared a National Treasure by the National Trust for Historic Preservation.

- **Tip 5: Value Your Brand**

Sarah married Charles Joseph Walker in 1905 after losing her husband and relocating to Louisiana to be with her brothers. Under her new alias, "Madam CJ Walker," she used her knowledge as a hairdresser to launch items such as "Madam Walker's Wonderful Hair Grower" and "Madam Walker's Vegetable Shampoo." As Madam CJ Walker, she grew her business from St. Louis to Denver to Pittsburgh and finally across the country.

- **Tip 6: Volunteering in the Community**

Walker established philanthropies, provided houses to the elderly, and became involved in the NAACP, the National Conference on Lynching, and other groups that aided African Americans from her new home in Harlem. When she died, she left two-thirds of her fortune to organizations that aided her neighborhood and people of color across the country.

- **Tip 7: Invest in Yourself**

Walker remained unfazed despite having difficulty finding investors for her Indianapolis factory. She put $10,000 of her own money into the Walker Manufacturing Company, making her the sole stakeholder, which paid off handsomely. She utilized her riches to purchase some substantial real properties, including a Harlem townhouse that was a popular hangout for Harlem Renaissance celebrities and a home in Irvington, N.Y., now a historical landmark.

Walker's legacy bet paid off. Her principles endure a century after her death. Her influence on the country, her industry, the growth of fairness in the workplace, and the lives of all women who worked with her is undeniable.

Her legacy will carry on for centuries if she uses her business as a vehicle to achieve the best with the resources she has created.

How can you use your business to its full potential as it grows?

What kind of legacy do you hope to leave behind?

We'll look at another extremely successful person whose leadership effect was enormous at the time.

John D. Rockefeller

John D. Rockefeller was born on the 8th of July, 1839, in New York. His father was a traveling salesman. The future oil magnate was a hard worker who started earning money as a youngster by tending to turkeys, selling candies, and helping neighbors. Following the Rockefeller family's 1853 relocation to Cleveland, Ohio, John completed his high school education and then briefly attended a commercial college to study bookkeeping. At age sixteen, he secured employment in 1855 as an office clerk for a commission company in Cleveland that purchased, marketed, and transported coal, grain, and other commodities. (He thought that September 26, the day he began the job and joined the corporate world, was so important that he celebrated this "job day" every year as an adult.) Rockefeller and a colleague founded their own commission company in 1859. In Titusville, Pennsylvania, the nation's first oil well was drilled in the same year. Rockefeller invested in a Cleveland refinery in 1863, together with a number of partners, to get into the then-burgeoning oil business.

Laura Celestia Spelman (1839–1915), an Ohio native whose father was a successful businessman, politician, and abolitionist involved in the Underground Railroad, was married to Rockefeller in 1864. (Her husband assisted in funding Spelman College, a historically black women's college in Atlanta, Georgia, which bears Laura Rockefeller's name.) The Rockefellers went on to produce five children: John D. Rockefeller, Jr., Edith Rockefeller McCormick, Elizabeth Rockefeller Strong, Alta Rockefeller Prentice, and Alice Rockefeller, who passed away at the age of thirteen months.

To acquire control of the refinery, which had grown to be the biggest in Cleveland, Rockefeller had to borrow money in 1865 and buy out some of his partners. He added additional business associates and broadened his ventures in the burgeoning oil sector throughout the ensuing years. Kerosene, a petroleum-based product used in lamps, was starting to become a basic necessity at the time. Along with Henry Flagler and a number of other entrepreneurs, including his younger brother William, Rockefeller founded the Standard Oil Company of Ohio in 1870. The president and major stockholder was John Rockefeller.

Standard Oil established a monopoly in the oil sector by acquiring competitors' refineries and creating businesses to sell and distribute its goods internationally. After these businesses merged in 1882, the Standard Oil Trust was formed, gaining control over 90% of the country's pipelines and refineries. Standard Oil did everything from constructing its own oil barrels to hiring scientists to find new applications for petroleum byproducts in an effort to take advantage of economies of scale.

Due to his immense riches and achievements, Rockefeller became a target for muckraking journalists, reform politicians, and other individuals who saw him as an example of corporate greed and disapproved of the strategies he had used to establish his empire. The New York Times stated in 1937 that "he was accused of building up enormous fortunes on the ruins of other men, getting rich on railroad rebates, bribing men to spy on competing companies, of making secret agreements, of forcing rivals to join the Standard Oil Company under threat of being forced out of business, and so on."

The first federal law to forbid trusts and combinations that restricted commerce was approved by the US Congress in 1890 and was known as the Sherman Antitrust Act. Two years later, the Supreme Court dissolved the Standard Oil Trust. Still, its activities were quickly absorbed by Standard Oil of New Jersey, which operated as a holding corporation. In 1911, the US Supreme Court declared that Standard Oil of New Jersey had violated antitrust laws and ordered its dismantling following years of litigation.

In the middle of the 1890s, Rockefeller left Standard Oil's daily activities. Inspired in part by fellow Gilded Age magnate Andrew Carnegie, who amassed a huge fortune in the steel industry before turning philanthropist and giving away most of his wealth, Rockefeller used the Rockefeller Foundation to donate over half a billion dollars to a variety of scientific, religious, and educational causes. Among his endeavors were the funding of the Rockefeller Institute for Medical Research (now Rockefeller University) and the University of Chicago.

In his private life, RNYfeller was an enthusiastic golfer, a temperance supporter, and a very religious man. His objective was to live to be 100 years old, but on May 23, 1937, at The Casements, his winter residence in Ormond Beach, Florida, he passed away at age 97.

The Secrets to John D. Rockefeller's Success

While some consider Rockefeller a criminal, others see him as a saint of charity. It would be more advantageous for business owners and executives to understand why he was so successful rather than categorizing him as either. I will share with you five leadership strategies that John D. Rockefeller used and that all entrepreneurs and executives may use.

- **Tip 1: Be Tenacious and Have a Plan to Reach Your Objectives.**

Resilience was one of John D. Rockefeller's most vital leadership qualities. He went above and beyond to achieve the goals he set for himself. His main life ambition as a youngster was to land a position at a reputable company. Following a ten-week college course, he created a strategy for the companies he would contact. However, the deck was stacked against him. Cleveland had a boom. The number of transplants from out of town seeking employment increased the population. When they could recruit an experienced worker, no rightful company owner would choose to offer a youngster a job. But giving up was not an option. Rockefeller desired freedom from "Devil Bill," his bigamist father. He would have to acquire a job since he had no other option.

At last, he was hired after entering the offices of produce commissaries Hewitt and Tuttle, and according to Rockefeller, this day summed up his life.

- **Tip 2: Having a Compelling "WHY" Factor**

John D. Rockefeller was unrelenting in pursuing wealth accumulation for a cause. He was a deeply pious guy who felt that God had given him the ability to make money so that he might assist the less fortunate. "Having been endowed with the gift I possess, it is my responsibility to earn money and utilize it for the betterment of society by my moral principles," Rockefeller stated in a William Hoster interview that was included in God's Gold. The business magnate really believed that God had endowed him with the capacity to make money, which he would then use to improve society. In Random Reminiscences of Men and Events, he remarked, "I know of nothing more disgusting and pitiful than a man who commits all the hours of the working day to make money to just have money."

Most of these multimillion-dollar donations were made to his charities, which included the General Education Board, Laura Spelman Rockefeller Memorial, Rockefeller Foundation, and Rockefeller Institute for Medical Research. Additionally, he supplied the funding for the Johns Hopkins School of Hygiene and Public Health and The University of Chicago. He financed scientific research that led to the development of meningitis and yellow fever vaccinations. In addition, he founded the RSC, an organization dedicated to curing hookworm, a disease that affected forty per cent of Southerners. In addition, Rockefeller's funds supported churches, expanded educational opportunities, trained medical personnel, and improved public health.

- **Tip 3: Think About Investment**

Thanks to Rockefeller's integration of waste-cutting and cost-saving measures, Standard Oil became a trillion-dollar company. He achieved this, among other things, by vertically integrating the business. By getting rid of third parties, costs were reduced. For instance, Rockefeller produced his barrels and supplied his wood rather than purchasing wooden ones for the storage or transportation of oil. The company lowered the oil price by assuming supply chain control. For example, 1860 saw the price of an oil barrel at $9.59. In 1890, the price dropped to $0.77. Standard Oil was able to increase output and eventually gain dominance in the market because it could save money.

- **Tip 4: Controlling Emotions and Feelings**

It was rumored that Rockefeller had a short fuse when he was younger. But as he grew older, he engaged in self-mastery exercises for all emotional regulation. He rose to the top due to two leadership traits: his quiet attitude and calm composure. "I had seen board meetings when excited men shouted profanity and made menacing gestures, but Mr. Rockefeller, maintaining the utmost courteous, controlled the room," one director said, according to Chernow. He prioritized harmony above all else, which frequently prompted him to make concessions.

- **Tip 5: Humility Despite Great Success**

Despite being the wealthiest man in the world at one point, Rockefeller exercised humility in leadership. He was known as "The Sponge" at work because he would go about the property with a notebook, asking his staff members questions and noting their responses. He was always seeking methods to improve the company, and regardless of their position, he respected the viewpoints of his employees and paid attention to what they had to say.

His executives liked him even more since he wasn't egotistical, which boosted his impact on them. He assigned Charles Pratt, with whom he most frequently disagreed, to take his place at the head of the boardroom table during meetings. Rockefeller took a seat toward the center of the table to blend in as the leader. Rather than commanding the space, he preferred to balance it.

John D. Rockefeller developed his innate people talents into leadership abilities throughout his life, which helped his business achieve remarkable success. He became one of the most well-known and prosperous business leaders of the 20th century by using his innate talents. Whether you like or dislike him, Rockefeller's life exemplifies what can happen when leaders collaborate with their greatest assets.

Thomas Edison

Edison is most known for inventing the incandescent light bulb, a technology designed to provide a commercially feasible and safe source of light inside. He also invented the phonograph and pioneered the American motion picture business. Edison was incredibly hardworking and automatically believed everyone should follow in his footsteps. He enjoyed aggressive rivalry, believing that other innovators only existed to be defeated by him. Edison's significance cannot be evaluated by the 1,093 patents he received or the wealth he amassed. Entering a room and turning on the light will help you understand it.

Thomas Edison's distinguishing personality qualities are perseverance, a love of technology, innovativeness, diligence, and independence.

On February 11, 1847, Thomas Alva Edison was born in the thriving port of Milan, Ohio, in the United States. He was the fourth of Samuel Ogden Edison, Jr. and Nancy Edison's seven sons to reach adulthood. His father was the son of a Loyalist fugitive who served as captain of the First Middlesex Regiment during the War of 1812. The family relocated from Nova Scotia to Ontario (then called Upper Canada). Samuel traveled the United States through Michigan and finally landed in Milan, Ohio, after participating in the failed Mackenzie Rebellion of 1837. The Edison patrilineal family line came from the Netherlands, and the surname was originally "Edeson." The family relocated to Port Huron, Michigan, when Thomas was born.

Thomas Edison was an extremely lively child in his youth. His constant questioning and apparent self-centered demeanor did not sit well with the other students at school. Thomas continued in school for almost 12 weeks before his overworked and irritable instructor lost patience with him. The teacher saw that Thomas Edison's forehead was significantly bigger than typical and labeled him a scatterbrained man. Thomas' hyperactive conduct exacerbated the problem, and his adored mother swiftly removed him from school after becoming aware of the situation. In a modern American situation, Thomas Edison may have been diagnosed with ADHD (attention deficit hyperactivity disorder) and given a medicine like Ritalin to keep him calm.

"My mother was the making of me," Thomas recounted. She was always honest and confident in me... And it always made me feel like I had someone to live for and that I couldn't let them down." An outstanding educator, Nancy Edison, opted to teach her son at home after becoming convinced that his vigorous personality and odd physical appearance were indicators of his extraordinary intelligence. R.G. Parker's scientific texts, the School of Natural Philosophy, and The Cooper Union for the Advancement of Science and Art provided Thomas with most of his early education.

Thomas Edison began selling sweets and newspapers on trains between Port Huron, Michigan, and Detroit when he was 12 years old after convincing his parents that he was ready to work. He later added veggies to the list, which helped boost his income. While Lincoln and Douglas were having public pre-Civil War discussions, Edison, who was 14 then, was busy utilizing his access to the daily accompanying press releases that were teletyped into the station. These words were published in his small newspaper, the Grand Trunk Herald.

Thomas' mini-publishing enterprise provided him with more than enough money to maintain himself. He'd spent much of his spare money on supplies for the chemical laboratory he'd set up in his parent's basement. His normally patient and easygoing mother ultimately protested about the stink and danger of all the chemical equipment, and he was compelled to relocate most of it to a secured room in the basement. The remainder was stored in a rail storage compartment.

The train lurched one day while traversing a rocky piece of track, and a stick of phosphorus rolled onto the floor and lighted up. The fire spread swiftly, and most baggage vehicles caught fire within minutes. The enraged conductor harshly chastised Thomas, smacking him in the side of the head with a strong punch. It is claimed that this was one of the causes of Edison's later serious hearing issues, the latter being scarlet fever and, less notably, mastoiditis. Following the event, the station masters prohibited Thomas from selling his newspaper at railroad stops along the track.

Telegraphy was influential in altering communication in America in the 1860s, and its possibilities soon enthralled Edison (who spent much of his time around train stations).

On a summer day in 1862, Edison was riding on a train when he noticed a boy running around the railroad tracks in front of an incoming boxcar. Thomas hurled himself at the poor child, shoving him and himself out of the path of the approaching train. The boy was the son of stationmaster James MacKenzie, who rewarded Edison's bravery by teaching him Morse code and how to use the telegraph.

Edison's first telegraphing work was as an operator for the local Western Union in Port Huron, thanks to MacKenzie's apprenticeship. Edison was still a newcomer and proved to be a poor message transmitter. He was just fifteen at the time and spent much of his shift learning about discipline and doing electrical and chemical experiments.

Many of Edison's early employment was lost due to his bad habits, and he spent the years between 1863 and 1867 traveling about the Midwest as a "tramp telegrapher." As he moved from city to city, he utilized his jobs mostly as laboratories for his experiments. It was referred to as "moonlighting" by him.

Edison was frequently dismissed for misbehaving or not being a good telegrapher. On one of these jobs in Indianapolis in 1864, Edison made what he said was his first genuine innovation. It was known as an "automatic repeater" and a gadget that allowed operators to interpret

Morse code messages at their own pace and convenience. He never patented the first version of the repeater.

Thomas A. Edison came home dirty and impoverished after four years on the road. It was 1868, and his mother's mental state was deteriorating, exacerbated by her frequently terrible existence. Samuel Edison Jr., his reckless father, had recently lost his job at the local bank, and the family was on the edge of poverty. Thomas had to confront the bleak tragedy of the situation, and after much soul-searching, he chose to get out on the road and try to return with a fortune.

Through a fellow telegrapher buddy, Edison found a position at a reasonably high-status Western Union Company in Boston within a few days. The relocation was partly influenced by a free railway ticket the local street railway operator provided in exchange for certain maintenance. Edison was en-route to Boston.

At the time, Boston was America's scientific and cultural epicenter, and Edison relished it. While working for Western Union, Edison frequently visited the Court Street workshop of Charles Williams Jr., a telegraph maker. The factory would be a gathering spot for Edison to trade equipment and ideas with like-minded persons. On October 11, 1868, Edison built his first patented innovation at the factory: an electric vote recorder for speeding up the voting process in the legislature by pushing one of two accessible buttons. On June 1, 1869, he received U.S. Patent 90,646.

The government promptly condemned the device, with a lawmaker informing Edison that if there was any invention he didn't want here, it was this one. The lawmakers wanted the opposite - time to alter the opinions of other legislators - and this technology contradicted their techniques. Edison needed money severely, and this event gave him an important lesson that would influence his naive view of business and marketing. Edison said that from now on, he would "never waste time inventing things that people would not want to buy."

Edison happened to lecture at Boston Tech during his 17-month stay in Boston. It was established in 1861 and changed its name to the Massachusetts Institute of Technology in 1916. Here, he was exposed to the brightest brains of his day, who were fiddling with communication technology and exploring the potential of the telegraph. Not unexpectedly, communication technology intrigued Alexander Graham Bell, who lived in Boston at the time. Bell's curiosity eventually inspired him to construct the first articulating telephone, directing Edison toward one of his most important innovations.

In Boston, Edison met the ambitious Benjamin Barnard Redding (January 17, 1824 - August 21, 1882), a Canadian-born California politician. Redding would later aid Alexander Graham Bell in perfecting long-distance telephony and in the production of the first reciprocating telephone and the magneto phone. Redding collaborated closely with notable promoter George B. Stearns, who bragged of getting the first patent for a duplex telegraph connection. Western

Union paid $750,000 for the patent. The technology piqued Edison's interest, and he traveled to Redding for a thorough explanation and knowledge of the multiplex transmitter system. Unlike Edison, Redding was quite modest and uninterested in bragging and self-promotion, which proved his undoing. The harsh survival of the fittest' world of patenting inventions in the mid-nineteenth century crushed Redding, only spurring the tough-minded Edison to work on improving the duplex transmitter, only to later come up with the world's first quadruplex transmitter system, which he then patented.

Edison's stay in Boston eventually left him significantly in debt and on the verge of being fired by Western Union for not being focused on the work and "doing too much moonlighting." Edison believed he would do better in a more business-focused environment, so he borrowed $35 from Benjamin Redding to buy a steamship ticket to New York City.

Edison was allegedly "on the verge of starving to death" shortly after landing in New York City. When things appeared to be becoming desperate, an incredible coincidence occurred.

While walking through New York's financial sector, Edison encountered a manager of a minor brokerage business who was panicking because a large stock ticker had just gone down in his office. Noticing that everyone else in the crowd had no idea how to fix it, he approached the scene and took advantage of the chance to try to repair the machine himself. Edison had been around for a few weeks and already had a solid concept of what this gadget was for. He reached down and replaced a single loose spring, and to everyone's surprise (save Edison's), the apparatus began to run flawlessly.

The office manager was so pleased that he gave Edison a repair position at the firm for $300 per month, more than twice the cost for a professional electrician in New York City. Edison subsequently describes the encounter as "almost surreal." He claimed to have been "suddenly delivered out of abject poverty and into prosperity within a few minutes."

Edison continued "moonlighting" with the telegraph and an updated version of the stock ticker in his spare time. When he first showed the world the upgraded stock ticker, the Gold and Stock Telegraph Company gave him $40,000 for all his rights to the gadget. He was taken aback by the figure, having expected little more than $5,000. He stretched out the money on his bed after cashing it in, counting it repeatedly in surprise. He heeded the counsel of a knowledgeable acquaintance, who advised him to put the money in a bank and forget about it for a while.

Edison spent a few years in New York, hopping from one company partnership to the next, mostly designing and producing telegraphic equipment and refining others' machinery. He primarily worked with written, automated, and multiplex telegraphs. These occupations gave him financial independence, allowing him to form two new enterprises with business partners in 1870. The company did not endure long, with Newark Telegraph Works closing in 1872 after the partner relocated to New York and American Telegraph Works being sold to Gold and Stock in 1871.

In 1870, Edison relocated to Newark, California, to manage several telegraph manufacturing operations, where he oversaw employees and earned a reputation as a tough boss. He worked on a contract with Gold and Stock in New York City until it was purchased by Western Union in 1871.

In Newark, Thomas Edison debuted the Quadruplex telegraph in 1874. A novel electrical telegraph allows the transmission and receiving of four independent signals on a single line at the same time. He was bound by an informal agreement to sell each of his innovation patents to Western Union. When Edison answered Western Union's inquiry about the progress of development, he informed them that he had sold his contract for the quadruplex telegraph to banker Jay Gould, igniting a court fight that would drastically alter Edison's contract with Western Union. After settling the legal issue in December 1875, Western Union provided Edison with a formal agreement, an assignment to construct an acoustic telegraph, and significant funds to fund his effort. He planned to utilize the funds to construct his ideal research center in Menlo Park, New Jersey, some 25 miles from New York City.

Thomas Edison established the Menlo Park laboratory in 1876. It is an important invention since it was the first institution to produce technical advancements. As Edison expressed it, the aim at Menlo Park was to generate a little idea every ten days and a substantial item every month or so. Although his subordinates carried out research and development under his direction, Edison was legally credited with most of the work from Menlo Park.

Edison was the only one with significant resources in the sector then. He would put a lot of pressure on his workers to generate outcomes. As a diligent man, he assumed that everyone should be like that. They frequently worked all night experimenting at the Menlo Park Laboratory and slept until midday. Edison is said to have kept track of how many hours he spent doing anything in a row and would aim to beat his record every time.

In the early 1870s, Edison's life was fast altering. His mother died in 1871, and on Christmas Day of that year, he married 16-year-old Mary Stilwell, whom he met while working at one of his subsidiaries, the News Reporting Telegraph Company in Newark. Mary came from a quiet and self-effacing Newark household.

They had three children by 1878: Marion Estelle Edison, known as "Dot," Thomas Alva Edison, Jr., known as "Dash," and William Leslie Edison. Mary's marriage was not an easy one. Edison was mostly away, working day and night at the Menlo Park Lab, leaving Mary to operate the house and care for the children. Thomas Edison couldn't afford to waste time since he knew his competition would quickly outpace him if he slowed down.

In July 1878, Edison and a handful of his helpers decided to go to the woods to observe an eclipse and escape the crowds of interested visitors and media at Menlo Park. Mary Edison, who was pregnant with their third child, William, was left behind. She stayed at home most of the time and was frequently unwell, suffering from headaches, panic attacks, and exhaustion. Her upbringing did not match Edison's objectives, and she soon discovered what it was like to marry a guy who was not present. While Edison was abroad, Mary became so unwell that she was placed under the continuous care of a doctor, and Edison was encouraged to return home immediately. He was gone for three weeks more, and when he returned, he went directly to the Menlo Park Laboratory.

The Centennial International Exhibition 1876, held in Philadelphia, Pennsylvania, marked the theatrical debut of America as the world's leading industrial force. There were innovations on display, ranging from a large steam engine capable of running 100 machines simultaneously to an elevator that assisted a man in climbing 11 levels while standing still, and from a typewriter to a sewing machine.

But no innovation was more remarkable than Alexander Grande Bell's telephone, which turned sound waves into electrical impulses. The technology was revolutionary in every respect, heralding a completely new mode of communication.

Edison had no regard for Bell and was eager to compete. To him, Bell was merely there to be beaten; as Edison once observed, "An inventor needs an enemy." The telephone became the subject of a patent battle between Bell and Elisha Gray, a Chicago electrical engineer who claimed to have created the underlying technology in 1874 after being displayed at the Centennial Exhibition in 1876. Bell won in the courts but faced market rivalry from Edison. While Bell attempted to replace the telegraph with the telephone, Western Union purchased Gray's telephone patent and immediately assigned Edison to develop Bell's system. Edison identified the flaw in the telephone's poor sound transmission. He devised the carbon button transmitter, which increased the loudness of the telephone and allowed it to become a commercially viable gadget.

Western Union benefited significantly from the Edison transmitter and used it with Gray's telephone receiver to sell the telephone under their name. After the apparatus was tested in England in 1878, Bell was enraged and vowed to prosecute Edison for patent violation. Edison attempted to create his receiver to avoid legal disputes, but his efforts were futile. Western Union eventually prompted a deal with Bell that gave him possession of Edison's carbon button transmitter. Edison, however, did not leave the telephone struggle empty-handed. His research with the equipment led him to discover an innovation that would permanently transform his life.

In the summer of 1877, Edison was working on improvements to Gray's telephone and the telegraph when he proposed employing a telephone diaphragm to create sound waves. He began experimenting with a diaphragm with an embossing point that was pressed against a quickly moving tinfoil-coated cylinder and created sound waves with the assistance of his crew. He also added two diaphragm-and-needle units to the machine, one for audio recording and the other for playback. When Edison spoke into a mouthpiece, the recording needle imprinted the sound vibrations onto the cylinder. "Mary had a little lamb" were Edison's first words in a mouthpiece. He was surprised that the phonograph had properly recorded them. After seven years of study, Edison concluded that to convince investors and make his phonograph economically feasible, he would need to employ the wax coating on the cylinder to increase the recording surface.

On August 12, 1877, Edison created the phonograph. Some historians believe it happened several months later since Thomas Edison only submitted a patent for the phonograph on December 24, 1877, and the patent was issued on February 19, 1878.

He established the Edison Speaking Phonograph Company on January 24, 1878, to commercialize the new machine. Edison received $10,000 for manufacturing and sales rights and 20% of the earnings.

Edison demonstrated the phonograph to members of Congress and the 19th US President, Rutherford B. Hayes, in the spring of 1878. Edison stood in for a portrait with Matthew Brady, a titan in photography, in April 1878. Suddenly, the Menlo Park Laboratory was inundated with visitors.

Thomas Edison proposed various applications for his created phonograph, including letter writing, phonographic books for blind people, music replication, music boxes and toys, educational objectives, and telephone connection to record conversations. Many of the recommended applications became a reality. Also, when the United States entered World War I in 1917, the Edison Company created a special version of the phonograph for the United States Army at $60.

It enabled soldiers to bring music to combat with them. Music was important to the troops since it could cheer them up and remind them of home. As a result, several Army units purchased phonographs to replay music.

In 1919, Edison even recorded his address, He expressed his gratitude to the troops and begged the American people to remember the sacrifices and contributions made by the other allied nations to bring about peace in "Let Us Not Forget - A Message to The American People," which he played on the phonograph.

The United States began to regard itself as a country of innovators in the late nineteenth century. It was almost as if an American would be humiliated if he died without a patent. Every week, The Scientific American would publish lists of new innovations and patent award announcements, and newspapers would write editorials about how the patent office symbolized American grandeur. The United States, formerly inferior to Europeans, was then a booming industrial powerhouse on the verge of revolutionizing the globe, and to flourish in this environment was to become a full-fledged superstar.

After understanding his social standing, Edison began to shape a 'colorful' public image of himself. He was never present to greet visitors at the Menlo Park Lab, always entering the room from 'elsewhere,' wearing his lab coat with a handkerchief around his neck and smudges on his face. Edison had a sense of humor and a deep belief in himself. People close to him characterized him as a good storyteller and a genius. Edison was viewed as a visionary and a magician by the general population.

However, by the late summer of 1878, Edison had begun the development of an electrical lighting system. He had an idea about how to make it, offered by a physicist acquaintance, and a few preliminary sketches in his notebook named "electric light." Edison began exploring ways to develop a long-lasting incandescent lamp that could be used inside.

By that time, American towns were lighted by two forms of light. Gas lighting had been used in households for some time, but its limitations were obvious. Aside from the risks of having an open flame in the house, gas lamps were dirty, smelled of acidic vapor, warmed rooms, and risked asphyxiation due to inadvertent leaks.

Arc lighting was the only commercial electric lighting technology available at the time. It was a mechanism that caused a current to bounce between two carbon rods, generating a blinding light that people typically shielded themselves from with umbrellas. The alternative was the incandescent light bulb, patented six years before Edison was born. The technology may be traced back to Alessandro Volta's demonstration of a blazing wire in 1800, which was improved upon by Sir Humphrey Davy, who first demonstrated 'incandescence' - an electric current running through a wire - in 1802. The main issue with incandescent lighting was developing a light bulb that would not burn out in seconds.

Since 1800, innovators on both sides of the Atlantic have been pondering how to construct a dependable electric lighting system. After a few days of exploratory trials, Edison was certain he had solved the problem. "Everyone will wonder how they never thought of it when it is known how I accomplished my goal," he said to a New York Sun reporter. It's rather simple."

Now and again, someone would tell the media, "Eureka! I've got it. But Edison was already in the public eye. Edison used his celebrity to his advantage, dominating headlines for a month after claiming to have invented an electric system that would reduce dependency on gas lighting. Gas stocks plummeted, and investors flocked to the Menlo Park Laboratory, willing to pay Edison any price for a project he had no idea would succeed.

Edison's previous telegraph knowledge enabled him to envision building a light. The most difficult challenge was locating acceptable filaments for the incandescent spiral and a bulb with a high resistance that could operate at a low power of 110 volts. On October 22, 1879, Edison felt they had made a breakthrough when the lamp with carbonized thread lasted 13.5 hours. On November 4, 1879, Edison applied for US patent 223,898 for the electric light, which used "a carbon filament or strip coiled and connected to platinum contact wires." This was the first commercially feasible incandescent lamp, granted on January 27, 1880.

Thomas Edison got US Patent No. 223,898 for Electric-Lamp on January 27, 1880.

The United States Patent and Trademark Office (USPTO) declared Edison's electric lamp patent invalid on October 8, 1883. According to the USPTO, it was based on the work of William E. Sawyer, an American inventor. It took Edison nearly six years, but on October 6, 1889, a judge declared that Edison's patent No. 223,898 for electric-light improvement was legitimate.

On November 27, 1880, Sir Joseph Wilson Swan, D.Sc.h.c., FRS, a British physicist and chemist, got a patent for creating the electric light bulb a year before Edison. To avoid a patent infringement fight with Joseph Swan, they merged the Swan United Electric Company with the Edison Electric Light Company in 1883 to become The Edison and Swan Electric Light Company Limited.

Along with a slew of litigation, Edison's personal life changed dramatically when his first wife, Mary Stilwell, died on August 9, 1884, presumably from a morphine overdose, leaving Edison a widower at the age of thirty-seven. Edison was surrounded by young women who offered him compassion since he was relatively young and had a considerable capital to his name. Mina Miller, a nineteen-year-old girl he met in the winter of 1885, captured his interest.

Mina, unlike Mary, grew up in a practical world and traveled a lot in social circles. Her father was an inventor, and she knew what it was like to be around famous people better than most women. Mina was self-sufficient and could follow her hobbies without clashing with Edison's 'big-shot' ego. Edison was taken aback by Mina and constantly wrote about her in his diary. He taught her Morse code so they could communicate in a crowded place by tapping each other on the hand. The two married on February 24, 1886, after he proposed to her similarly.

The same year, Edison and Mina relocated to their new home, Glenmont, in Llewellyn Park in West Orange, New Jersey. That was his wedding present for Mina. In addition, in 1885, Thomas Edison purchased Seminole Lodge in Fort Myers, Florida, which became their winter hideaway. There, the pair spent many winters together.

Thomas Edison and Mina Miller had three children: Madeleine Edison, Charles Edison, and Theodore Miller Edison, who has over 80 patents.

Edison was ready to return to his ambitions when his personal life was fully established. Edison moved his brilliant crew to his new laboratory in Orange, New Jersey, on November 24, 1887. He bragged that it was the best-equipped and largest laboratory in the world, occupying a section of Main Street near his new home. As Edison put it, this 21-acre building housed "everything from cowhide to the eyeballs of a United States senator." In contrast to the Menlo Park Laboratory, the new institution focused on production and business rather than creation. This would be the start of Edison's career as a commercial businessman. Nonetheless, the West Orange Laboratory produced key discoveries such as the Kinetoscope (an early motion picture presentation device), the motion picture camera, the dictating machine, sound recordings, and better phonographs.

During his tenure at West Orange Lab, Edison was also working on developing the phonograph when an old rival, Alexander Graham Bell, unveiled the Graphophone. This invention was primarily reliant on Edison's technology. Thomas Edison received more than eighty patents on enhancements to the cylinder phonograph during his first four years at the West Orange lab. Edison sold the improved photograph's marketing rights for $500,000 to an entrepreneur who struck an under-the-table agreement with Edison's then-close friend and colleague, George Ezra Gilliland. When Edison discovered that Gilliland stood to profit $250,000 from the purchase, he cancelled Gilliland's contract, considering it an act of total betrayal.

Thomas Edison approached Jenkins and Armat and offered to buy the patent rights to their gadget. Jenkins and Armat had no option but to comply since they realized they would never be able to compete with Edison because everyone in the industry expected Edison to create a new machine. Edison purchased the Phantascope patent rights from Jenkins and Armat on the condition that the gadget be presented as a new Edison innovation named Vitascope. The Vitascope premiered on April 23, 1896, at Koster and Bial's Music Hall in New York City, displaying quality pictures on a 203-foot screen and effectively beginning the American Motion Picture Industry in Edison's name.

The motion picture industry quickly became a hot market. By 1900, there were around 500 court proceedings on patent claims related to the motion picture business due to the many innovators involved in improving the technology. As a result, in December 1908, The Motion

Picture Patents Company (MPPC) was established. The MPPC sought to improve profitability for all industry participants. Despite criticism from independent firms for monopolism, it was liquidated in 1918. Thomas Edison was forced out of the market due to falling pricing and competition. In 1918, Edison sold his stake in the MPPC to the Lincoln and Parker Film Company.

Thomas Edison approached Jenkins and Armat and offered to buy the patent rights to their gadget. Jenkins and Armat had no option but to comply since they realized they would never be able to compete with Edison because everyone in the industry expected Edison to create a new machine. Edison purchased the Phantascope patent rights from Jenkins and Armat on the condition that the gadget be presented as a new Edison innovation named Vitascope. The Vitascope premiered on April 23, 1896, at Koster and Bial's Music Hall in New York City, displaying quality pictures on a 203-foot screen and effectively beginning the American Motion Picture Industry in Edison's name.

The motion picture industry quickly became a hot market. By 1900, there were around 500 court proceedings on patent claims related to the motion picture business due to the many innovators involved in improving the technology. As a result, in December 1908, The Motion Picture Patents Company (MPPC) was established. The MPPC sought to improve profitability for all industry participants. Despite criticism from independent firms for monopolism, it was liquidated in 1918. Thomas Edison was forced out of the market due to falling pricing and competition. In 1918, Edison sold his stake in the MPPC to the Lincoln and Parker Film Company.

Edison's career would come to an end in the 1920s. Public service had become less important to him than spending time with his family. He started going home for supper and discovered a wonderful buddy in his wife, Mina. Following his father's death, Edison groomed his son, Charles Edison, to lead Thomas Edison Inc.

He was also frequently seen with Henry Ford, who saw Edison as a role model. They had similar hobbies, frequently discussing automobiles, and even conducted a series of gypsy car journeys throughout the United States, frequently attracting the attention of the press. Edison pushed Ford to keep working on the electric vehicle, which he saw as the future of transportation.

On October 18, 1931, Thomas Edison passed away in New Jersey. At the time, he was 84 years old. Edison created a tremendous legacy that cannot be assessed in terms of the 1,093 patents he received or spent throughout his lifetime. Shortly before his departure, he awoke from a coma and remarked to his wife, sitting by his side all night, "It is very beautiful over there..." His final breath is said to be kept at the Henry Ford Museum. Soon after Edison died, Ford allegedly convinced Edison's son Charles to collect a sample of air from Edison's chamber and put it in a test tube. Mina Edison, his loving wife, died on August 24, 1947.

Edison's remains rested in the West Orange Public Library for two days as over 50,000 people came to pay their last respects to the man whose intellect lifted the globe out of darkness. On the third night, US President Herbert Hoover addressed radio listeners across the country, asking them to dim or turn off their lights in unison - nearly an apocalyptic scenario reminding the world what life would have been like without Edison.

Secrets of Thomas Edison's Success

If you didn't know the story of Thomas Edison before, now you do. Many years after his death, his innovations and their current importance in our world.

But did you know he landed in New York from Boston (USA), friendless and deeply in debt due to his unsuccessful attempts there? I came upon an old interview of his in which he discussed the ideas that contributed to his success in life, business, and as a leader.

I've decided to share those concepts with you because they're just as valid now as they were back then, and they'll assist you a lot on your path to success.

- **Tip 1: Being Poor and Hungry is a Blessing**

When asked if hunger and need could drive a person to achievement, Thomas Edison replied, "It certainly makes him keep a sharp lookout." "I believe it moves a man along."

This remark completely resonates with me. I, too, feel that being broke and hungry is a godsend since it forces you to go above and beyond to do whatever is legitimate to improve your circumstances.

Rather than complaining about your current situation, use it as fuel to propel you forward.

- **Tip 2: Prepare to Work Hard Hours to Attain Your Objectives**

How diligently do you pursue your desires and goals? In my experience, most people cannot devote sufficient time to pursuing their objectives and goals. Working from 8 a.m. to 4 p.m. or 9 a.m. to 5 p.m. will usually only earn you a livelihood. To grow your business and achieve great success, you must be willing to labor past 5 p.m.

Thomas Edison stated that he worked 20 hours a day for 15 years. While it may seem severe, that is how much time he devoted to being who he is to us and carving his name in the tablet of immortality.

- **Tip 3: Success is Not the Consequence of Chance or Luck**

It always surprises me how many individuals rely on good fortune or luck to help them achieve success. Today, far too many individuals take the easy way out. They don't want to take any chances, so they sit and pray and hope everything will work out.

Thomas Edison was asked whether his discoveries and inventions occurred to him while he was sleeping. He stated, "Except for the phonograph, I never did anything worthwhile by accident, nor did any of my inventions come indirectly through accident." No, when I'm certain that the outcome is worthwhile, I go about it, trial after trial, until it occurs."

Consider this. How many times are you willing to attempt and try again till you achieve your objectives? Do you even have objectives?

- **Tip 4: Love What You Do - It Mustn't Be About Money**

"What motivates you to work?" was posed to Thomas Edison. What drives you to this never-ending struggle? What have you demonstrated that you do for the money it brings you?" "I like it," he said. There are no additional causes that I know of."

What about you? Why do you do what you do? Do you enjoy your job? Consider your response. If you don't enjoy what you do, you'll give up when you learn that the success or money you expected doesn't arrive as soon or in the volume you expected.

- **Tip 5: Concentrate on One Thing at a Time**

A lack of attention is one of the primary reasons most individuals are unproductive. They take on too many projects at once and, as a result, cannot execute them well.

Throughout his brilliant career, Thomas Edison began his day at 7 a.m. and went to bed at 11 p.m. "If you get up at seven o'clock in the morning and go to bed at eleven o'clock at night, you've put in sixteen good hours, and most guys have surely been doing this all the time."

They've either been strolling, reading, working, or thinking. The only problem is that they do many things while I just do one. They would succeed if they devoted the time to the issue in one way, to one topic. The problem is that people don't have an object to which they may cling, letting everything else go."

These are invaluable success ideas that are still very much applicable today. Which of these rings true for you? Please share your thoughts on the review page.

Sam Walton

Sam Walton is an American businessman, entrepreneur, and the creator of Walmart. Thomas Gibson Walton and Nancy Lee gave birth to him on March 29, 1918, in Kingfisher, Oklahoma. Sam Walton wanted to serve his country by joining the United States Army Intelligence Corps. He was Captain and served in Salt Lake City, Utah. Sam spent three years in the military.

Sam Walton intended to create a discount business after returning from the service. He made certain that fresh supplies were constantly on the shelves. He launched the shop with a $20,000 loan from his father-in-law and $ 5,000 saved while serving in the military.

In 1945, Sam Walton leased a branch of the Ben Franklin shop. He aimed to sell things cheaply to increase sales while maintaining a low profit margin. The business was a success when it first opened, with an annual income of $105,000, and by the fifth year, it had increased to $250,000.

The lease expired after five years, and Sam Walton could not extend it, forcing him to close the business. Walton's Five and Dime was the name he gave to his new business in Bentonville. This location is currently known as the Walmart Museum.

The first actual Walmart shop debuted in Rogers, Arkansas on July 2, 1962. It was known as the Wal-Mart Discount Store, and Sam Walton's purpose was to stock the store with solely American-made goods and offer them at a low price. Sam made certain that his

144

businesses were not just located in large cities but also in little communities.

On October 31, 1969, the firm formed under the name Wal-Mart Inc., which was later changed to Wal-Mart Stores Inc. in 1970. The next year, Walmart began trading stocks and was listed on the New York Stock Exchange. The price per share was $47 on the initial stock split in May 1971.

In 1974, the businesses expanded into Tennessee, Mississippi, and Kentucky. When the corporation first entered Texas, it had 125 locations, 7,500 workers, and $340.3 million in revenue.

In the 1980s, Walmart had been in business for 25 years and was quickly expanding. The corporation has 1198 locations, over 200,000 employees, and a $15.9 billion yearly revenue.

The globe was suffering from the effects of the COVID-19 epidemic in the 2020s, so Walmart announced some additional employee benefits. Employees can now stay home and take unpaid leave if they are ill or feel unsafe coming to work. If the workers contract the Covid-19 virus, they will be paid for up to two weeks. Walmart is the world's largest private employer, employing 2.2 million people.

The wedding of Sam Walton and Helen Robson took place on February 14, 1943. The couple's four children were Samuel Robson, John Thomas, James Carr, and Alice Louise.

Sam Walton died on April 5, 1992, in Little Rock, Arkansas, from blood cancer. He bequeathed Walmart ownership to his wife and children, and Samuel Walton replaced him as Chairman of Walmart.

The Secrets of Sam Walton's Success

- **Tip 1: Commitment**

He stated that you must trust your business more than anyone else's. And he demonstrated it because no one believed he could achieve in the manner that he did. You will not be able to work the hours required to reach your goals if you do not have a strong love for what you do.

- **Tip 2: Profit Sharing with Employees**

Everyone who has worked in a company knows that their most valuable asset is their workforce. Walton understood that if he could compromise them, he would be one step closer to success.

- **Tip 3: Applaud What the "Associates" Do.**

Sam phoned his colleagues, emphasizing that both worked to move the firm ahead and profited from their efforts. He was continually emphasizing the importance of appreciating good work.

- **Tip 4: Comment**

Without a doubt, one of Walton's secrets was that he monitored consumer behavior in his supermarkets and altered store layouts to optimize the shopping experience.

- **Tip 5: Going Against the Tide**

Although this did not always succeed, Walton was certain that doing what no one else was doing was one of the keys to his success. In your instance, set cheap pricing with a small profit margin.

- **Tip 6: Keeping Losses Under Control**

The company's fundamental idea is to help its consumers save money by shopping at supermarkets.

- **Tip 7: Outstanding Customer Service**

The consumer was in charge for Sam, and if he could meet his expectations, he would return to his supermarkets.

Bill Gates

Bill Gates was born on October 28, 1955, in Seattle, Washington. William Gates, Sr., and Mary Maxwell Gates are his parents. Gates' father was a local lawyer, and his mother was involved in several community organizations and banks. Gates has frequently addressed the good outcomes of his childhood and how they contributed to his success in life. Both probably affected his academic progress and contributed to his exceptionally high IQ.

Gates was born into a household of five, including an elder sister and a younger sister. Growing up, his family was characterized as "relatively close."

Gates demonstrated an early interest in computers. He aspired to be a lawyer like his father when he was younger, but that changed as he became more familiar with computers.

This passion intensified after his prep school's Mothers' Club purchased computing equipment. Gates began to build programs in several computing languages, collaborating with friends to broaden his understanding of how computers functioned.

Gates was little for his age, and his lower stature caused him to be teased as a youngster. While his height would eventually grow to 5"10', it caused several problems for Gates as a youngster. He subsequently stated that his little stature - and ensuing bullying - helped shape him into the leader he is today. Gates also ascribed his bullying to his extremely high intelligence, which he attributed to his above-average IQ.

Gates' first business endeavor began when he was 17 years old when he joined up with a buddy to launch a firm that manufactured traffic counts. Of course, this was just a taste of what was to follow.

Gates excelled academically and enrolled at Harvard in 1973. This was no surprise to anyone who knew Gates, given his economic success and exceptionally high IQ (estimated to be 160). He met Steve Ballimer while there. The two struck an immediate friendship.

Bill Gates founded Microsoft in June 1975 as a software development business. Despite the efforts of its team members, the firm first had challenges in selling software goods. Because the firm did not have enough funds to hire a professional sales manager, Bill Gates' mother, Mary Maxwell Gates, filled this role.

Early the next year, Gates and Allen noticed that the company's income had fallen to its most affordable level. Its major motive was 'piracy,' or software's illicit copying and usage without the creator's consent. Many individuals copied MS Basic and passed it on to others. When Bill Gates realized this, he became enraged, mostly because 'piracy' robbed him of a well-earned salary. Furthermore, these copies had certain errors he wished to eliminate before the official release of MS Basic. In February 1976, Gates released an open letter in an Altair newsletter. The Gates Foundation got 300 responses, but a few included a check.

Bill Gates was the first to recognize the need for software security. His activities have significantly contributed to the eventual acceptance of the idea that a computer program is a product of creativity and, as such, must be protected in the same way that a musical composition or a literary work is.

In 1976, it became clear that Bill Gates could not complete his studies while still managing a burgeoning corporation. Despite his parents' misgivings, he quit university in December and became totally immersed in the business. He was only twenty-one years old at the time.

The young businesspeople then struck gold, and Microsoft's sales profit surpassed $500,000 in the 1977 fiscal year. The firm, situated in Albuquerque, New Mexico, employed 13 individuals. Paul Allen and

Bill Gates were involved in organizational issues: Paul was in charge of creating new software, while Bill negotiated with computer manufacturers and oversaw the company's day-to-day operations.

Bill received an offer from IBM in 1979 to develop an operating system for the world's first personal computer. However, Bill Gates was compelled to reject IBM's approach because he had no OS designs. As a result, Microsoft's CEO was obliged to advise IBM to seek assistance from its competitor, Digital Research, which subsequently became the creator of the operating system for IBM's personal computer.

Meanwhile, Microsoft purchases a 'crude' operating system, 86-DOS, from Seattle Computer for $50,000 and recruits Tim Paterson, the developer of 86-DOS. Bill Gates' team greatly improved 86-DOS, and the world soon saw MS-DOS, which Microsoft offered to use as the principal operating system for IBM personal computers, thus defeating Digital Research. IBM signed a specific deal with Microsoft in September 1980. This transaction was intended to alter the course of the personal computer industry's history. It helped both IBM and Microsoft. Digital Research, Gates' major opponent, changed the company's path and was no longer active in the battle.

Microsoft established a business in 1981, with Bill Gates and Paul Allen sharing control. The next year, IBM released their personal computer with the 16-bit operating system MS-DOS. The IBM PC also incorporates Microsoft programs such as BASIC, COBOL, Pascal, and others.

In 1982, Gates persuaded IBM management that MS-DOS should be supplied under license to other computer makers, thereby eliminating Apple's competitor, which was selling machines based on its operating system.

The Microsoft Hardware department designed the 'Mouse' manipulator in 1983 for quick data entry into a computer with a graphical user interface. The business also released a text editor for MS-DOS the same year. Bill Gates also launched Windows, an expansion of the MS-DOS operating system that serves as a universal working environment for visual programs.

1986, Microsoft entered the IPO market, and one share cost increased from $22 to $28 in a single day. Microsoft has subsequently begun to control an entire sector, owning around 44 per cent of all earnings in the software market. It also stifled the growth of other businesses. In an interview in 1991, Lotus Development Corp. founder Mitch Kapor claimed, "The revolution is over, and the free-wheeling innovation in the software industry has ground to a halt." It's the Kingdom of the Dead for me."

The Secrets of Bill Gates' Success

Bill Gates exemplifies the value of dedication, hard work, teamwork, practice, and sound decision-making in reaching success. Whether you succeed or fail, don't be scared to get back up and try again. Gates was previously unable to recruit team members due to a lack of cash, but today has a net worth of $90.6 billion and lives a thriving life as one of the world's richest men. I'll share some of the keys to his success as a company leader with you here.

- **Tip 1: The Desire to Do Something**

Since he was in eighth grade, Bill Gates has been attracted by technology and programming. The Mothers Club at Bill Gates' school purchased a Teletype Model 33, which he had access to years before other schools had computers.

Bill Gates' fascination with computers fueled his drive to learn more about their software and hardware, and he offered to assist his school in identifying computer problems.

- **Tip 2: Practice Brings Perfection**

Later, pupils, including Bill Gates, violated the security procedures on their school's computers, resulting in a system ban. Following the restriction, Bill Gates made an offer to CCC and three of his friends to find flaws in the software in exchange for more computer time, which CCC accepted.

Bill Gates and his team worked with CCC to help with defect detection. Because of their expertise in computer languages, they were able to perfect programming. Bill Gates polished his skills via constant practice, a lesson everyone pursuing success may benefit from.

- **Tip 3: Decision Making**

At age 17, Bill Gates had to decide if he wanted to follow his programming love. With his close friend and business partner Paul Allen, he launched Traf-O-Data, a firm specializing in traffic-counting systems and data delivery for traffic engineers.

Bill Gates and Paul Allen commissioned MITS in 1975 to create a minicomputer emulator to implement the BASIC programming language. Microsoft, their company, was founded during that time. Starting a new company was a tremendous risk, but Gates and Allen were helped by good timing and a business strategy.

- **Tip 4: Work Hard, Don't Give Up**

In 1980, Microsoft's sales were uncertain, and the company was on a tight budget and couldn't afford to hire a sales manager. But Gates refused to give up. Bill Gates took a detour from his Harvard studies to work on Microsoft at the time.

They chose to quit MITS and focus only on Microsoft, improving its products and services. It was a breakthrough event for Microsoft when it licensed an operating system called MS-DOS to be used on IBM's personal computers, a computing juggernaut at the time. As a result, Microsoft has surpassed Apple as the world's leading supplier of operating systems.

- **Tip 5: Teamwork**

Bill Gates was never one to work alone; he co-founded Microsoft with his friend Paul Allen and eventually oversaw a team of individuals. He read every code sold at Microsoft's inception. Bill Gates was enthusiastic about Microsoft and wanted his employees to be as well. Working in a group rather than alone makes achieving achievement simpler.

- **Tip 6: Determination**

It wasn't an easy road, and Microsoft worked hard to broaden its product offerings as much as possible. Bill Gates was a success, but he found himself at the forefront of consumer software development and information technology, where he faced fierce competition from a flood of enterprises eager to capitalize on a rising market.

Bill Gates' success is a monument to the power of perseverance, resilience, and lifelong learning. His experience with Microsoft serves as an example for aspiring leaders, entrepreneurs, and innovators. Leaders and prospective leaders may aim to achieve amazing leadership success by embracing failure, being devoted to their goal, and cultivating a strong support structure, much like Bill Gates did. Make Bill Gates your inspiration, and let his tale inspire you to strive for excellence in your undertakings.

Jeff Bezos

Jeffrey Bezos was born on the 12th of January, 1964, in Albuquerque, New Mexico. Ted Jorgenson, Jeff's real father, was a top unicyclist in Albuquerque and a member of the Unicycle Wranglers, a local company that performed at county fairs and circuses when Jeff was a baby. Jeff's mother, Jacklyn Bezos, married Ted when she was still in her teens, and their marriage lasted a little over a year.

Mike Bezos, Jeff's stepfather, was born in Cuba. At age 15, he fled to the United States and began working at the University of New

Mexico. When Mike married Jeff's mother, the family relocated to Houston, Texas, where Mike worked as an engineer for Exxon-American, a successful oil and gas business from the mid-1940s until the 1970s.

Jeff had extraordinary mechanical skills from a young age, corresponding to his diverse scientific interests. He had dismantled his cot with a screwdriver as a kid, and as a teen, he had created an electronic alarm to keep younger siblings out of his room. Jeff's parents finally persuaded him to relocate all his belongings to their garage, which he transformed into a laboratory for his research pursuits.

Jeff's mother's relatives were early immigrants in Texas, and the family possessed a big ranch near Cotulla that had been passed down through the years. Lawrence Preston "Pop" Gise, Jeff's grandpa, was a regional director of The United States Atomic Energy Commission (AEC) in Albuquerque and oversaw the Los Alamos and Lawrence Livermore nuclear facilities before retiring to the family ranch.

Jeff Bezos went to Houston's River Oaks Elementary School for his fourth and sixth grades. He would spend his summers at the ranch doing activities as diverse as installing piping, repairing windmills, vaccinating livestock, and other farm labor. Lawrence Gise, his grandpa, was a great role model for him, with his broad scientific knowledge and regular presence on the ranch. In a 2010 commencement speech, Jeff warned graduates that "it's harder to be kind than it is to be clever."

Bezos established his first firm while still in high school. The Dream Institute was a summer educational camp for fourth--, fifth--, and sixth-grade students. Bezos required his volunteers to read certain novels. They were J. R. R. Tolkien's The Lord of the Rings novel, Frank Herbert's Dune novel, Robert A. Heinlein's Stranger in a Strange Land novel, T. H. White's The Once and Future King novel, Richard Adams' Watership Down novel, Anna Sewell's Black Beauty novel, Jonathan Swift's Gulliver's Travels novel, Charles Dickens' David Copperfield novel, and Robert Louis Stevenson's Treasure Island novel.

When the family relocated to Florida, Jeff was transferred to Miami Palmetto Senior High School, where he excelled academically and discovered his passion for computer. He was even accepted to the University of Florida's Student Science Training Program, where he received a Silver Knight Award and was a National Merit Scholar in 1982. Bezos graduated as valedictorian and a National Merit Scholar, gaining his place at Princeton University.

Bezos had planned to study physics at Princeton University, but he soon changed his mind and returned to his first passion, computers. He earned two Bachelor of Science degrees in computer science and electrical engineering from Princeton University. "Middle-of-the-road theoretical physicists make no progress." "They spend all of their time understanding other people's progress," Bezos said of his choice to the Guardian.

After graduation, Bezos headed to Wall Street, where computer science was in high demand, and worked for several corporations. Every week, he flew between New York and London for his employment at Fitel (a company seeking to develop a network to conduct international trade).

Bezos remained in finance, rising to vice president with Bankers Trust and eventually with the investment firm D.E. Shaw. Bezos was selected for his general expertise in the industry and the business, specializing in bringing computer sciences to the stock market. Jeff met his wife, MacKenzie, a Princeton graduate at D.E. Shaw. In 1993, Jeff married MacKenzie Bezos. Bezos climbed swiftly up the ranks, becoming the company's youngest senior vice president in 1990.

Jeff Bezos discovered a digit at D.E. Shaw that would transform his life and the path of internet history. Bezos saw a figure about the World Wide Web increasing at 2,300 per cent per month while scanning the Web for new enterprises for D.E. Shaw. Bezos saw the potential benefits of selling items online right away. On a long stroll around Central Park, Shaw attempted to persuade Bezos to stay with his company, but Jeff chose to try and fail rather than never try.

Bezos left D.E. Shaw in 1994 and relocated to Seattle to capitalize on the Internet market's promise by starting an online bookshop. He created a list of things he might offer online, such as CDs, software, and hardware. Because of the variety of titles, books were ultimately the logical choice. Another advantage of an online business was a recent U.S. Supreme Court decision that mail-order catalogs did not have to pay taxes in places without physical presence. In other words, Bezos paid no taxes on the goods he sold online.

Because of Seattle's large pool of high-tech expertise at that time, Bezos believed it would be an ideal location for his new venture. While his wife MacKenzie drove them from Texas, he worked on a business plan on his laptop and contacted potential investors. Jeff Bezos raised $1 million from relatives and friends to start his company in the garage of his Seattle home.

On July 5, 1994, Bezos incorporated the firm as "Cadabra". However, a year later, when his lawyer misheard the term "cadaver," he pondered altering it, but it was not the worst of it. Another option was "MakeItSo.com," a tagline from Jeff's favorite Star Trek series. It might alternatively have been "aard.com," which would have pushed the firm to the top of search engine results. Jeff and MacKenzie also registered Awake.com, Browse.com, Bookmall.com, and Relentless.com (the latter still link to Amazon.com). After perusing the dictionary for terms beginning with the letter A, Bezos settled on Amazon.com. Bezos appreciated the parallel between one of the world's longest rivers and the world's largest bookshop.

Jeff and MacKenzie set up everything in their two-bedroom house, with extension wires going down to the garage and three Sun micro stations on tables Jeff built out of $60 doors. Ironically, staff meetings would take place in the local Barnes & Noble bookshop. When everything was finished, Jeff and MacKenzie gathered 300 individuals to test the site once it was up and running, and the code functioned flawlessly across many computer systems. They encouraged their 300 test users to spread the news and set up a bell to ring every time Amazon made a sale after launching the website on July 16, 1995. The Bell stayed there for a month before Amazon blossomed, selling books in all 50 states and 45 foreign nations. By September 1995, weekly sales had reached $20,000 a week.

Bezos was determined to take the firm public through an IPO and hired many employees. A few DESCO personnel were among them: officials from competitor firm Barnes & Noble, software giant Symantec, and two Microsoft employees - vice president of engineering Joel Spiegel and David Risher, who would eventually become head of retail. With a team of remarkable people in his top leadership ranks (dubbed the J-Team), Bezos was certain that "if we get this right, we might be a $1 billion company by 2000."

He reasoned that going public would strengthen consumer trust and enable Bezos to compete with rival booksellers that would shortly launch their own online. The most prominent competitor was Barnes & Noble. Between 1991 and 1997, they established 'the book superstore,' putting small independent bookshops out of business and revolutionizing bookselling. Their revenues were expected to exceed $2 billion in 1996, while Amazon lags with $16 million the same year.

The Riggio brothers, Leonard and Steve Riggio, who controlled Barnes & Noble, traveled to Seattle to meet with Bezos and Tom Alberg, founder and managing partner of the venture capital company Madrona Venture Group and a director of Amazon.com. Knowing

Leonard Riggio's character - a tough-as-nails Bronx businessman dressed in an expensive suit with a passion for fine art - the team opted for a cautious and flattering approach. The Riggios came on strong and menacing, announcing their intention to launch their website, eliminating Amazon from the market. They proposed a variety of cooperation, including creating a website and licensing Amazon's technology. Bezos and Alberg agreed they'd think about it over dinner, but following a phone call, they realized this combination would not work.

While the Riggios were at home building their website, Jeff Bezos and Amazon's first CFO, Joy Covey, toured the United States and Europe to present Amazon to possible investors. They had a solid foundation, with millions in sales in their first three years and a readily accessible single warehouse and inventory, unlike other merchants with wares distributed around the country. They also employed a 'negative operating cycle,' meaning buyers paid using credit cards when the product came, but Amazon settled its debts with wholesalers every several months. Almost every investor inquired whether the two would expand into other categories, and Bezos said they had settled on books. He wanted to acquire some IPO financing but didn't want his competitors to follow in his footsteps by hiding a lot of vital info from investors. Everyone assumed that once Barnes & Noble entered the market, Amazon would be "Amazon Toast."

Barnes & Noble sued Amazon in federal court on May 12, 1997, three days before the IPO, for fraudulently claiming to be "Earth's

Largest Bookstore." It happened during the SEC-mandated seven-week "quiet period," which meant Bezos couldn't speak to the press before the IPO. Surprisingly, the case just drew greater attention to Amazon. The two firms clashed aggressively for about a year after Amazon went public. Barnes & Noble had a larger catalog, but Amazon attempted to locate books from small dealers and antique stores. Barnes & Noble received a $200 million investment from German media conglomerate Bertelsmann and went public. Bezos then quickly extended Amazon's product range and renamed it "Books, Music, and More," leaving Barnes & Noble "wrapping its arms around the neck of a phantom," as one writer described it.

The stock originally traded below its IPO price, and Bezos was concerned that the business would lose a major chunk of its investment. On the IPO day, May 15, 1997, the stock price was fixed for a $12-to-$14 range on NASDAQ (AMZN). The price then rose from $14 to $16 until Amazon's investment bankers agreed on $18. Amazon.com received $54 million in its first public offering (IPO), and the online bookstore's market valuation hit $438 million. Amazon is selling 3 million shares. Amazon had a record-breaking year, with yearly revenue increasing by 900 per cent. Bezos' family had each put $10,000 as a backup plan - a sizable portion of their life savings. By the end of the decade, they formally became multimillionaires as six per cent owners of Amazon, and Jeff was awarded Time's Person of the Year in 1999.

eBay began as a Silicon Valley firm on September 03, 1995, under AuctionWeb. Unlike Amazon, eBay was profitable and growing, which made it a formidable competitor. The company's revenue increased to $224.7 million in 1999 from $5.7 million in 1997 and $47.4 million in 1998. The business plan was ideal: eBay charged a little commission for each transaction, but since sellers were individuals offering their goods for auction to the highest bidder, there was no need for warehouses, postal services, or inventory storage. Although the website began with baseball cards and memorabilia, it was quickly moving toward being the "unlimited selection" store that Bezos had long desired.

In the summer of 1998, after eBay filed to go public, Bezos brought the company's founder, Pierre Omidyar and CEO Meg Whitman to Seattle (IPO). The two executive teams, who would see each other frequently over the following ten years, talked about different approaches to collaboration. Omidyar and Whitman proposed linking products so that, for instance, customers would be sent to Amazon.com if the product was unavailable on eBay.com and vice versa. Bezos' suggestion of making a sizable investment turned the two executives off because they believed he was making an offer to purchase eBay Inc. for around $600 million. Though official proposals were not made, the figure was close to the market valuation that eBay was aiming for during its first public offering. Omidyar remembers being shocked by employees with body piercings and tattoos while on tour at the Dawson Street distribution center. He was also pleased by the facility's automation. Whitman told Omidyar to "get over it," not seeming impressed. This is rather awful. Handling warehouses in this manner is the last thing we want to do. Like Bezos, eBay executives were initially incredibly ambitious and believed they were creating a whole new kind of virtual commerce. Trying to persuade them differently would be fruitless. Bezos's well-known, unique chuckle turned many off as well.

Once he could not reach an agreement with the executives, Bezos secretly tried to launch his auction idea. The initiative, known as EBS, or "Earth's Biggest Selection," was based on the second floor of Columbia Center. By spring, staff joked that it was eBay. Amazon Auctions had a sluggish opening at its debut in March 1999. Bezos began investing much time, money, and attention into the project. He bought a firm to stream live auctions online and joined Sotheby's Auction House to concentrate on luxury goods. The entire endeavor was pointless. Consumers used to traditional retail and fixed pricing might discover Amazon Auctions via a link on the company's main website, only to find themselves in a seedy second-hand leftovers market.

Although the 1990s were a demanding period for the firm, according to Jeff Blackburn, who oversees operations and product development at Amazon, they were also the most enjoyable and difficult. Bezos's "uplifting" loss was attributed to the network effect, which states that its value increases when more people utilize an item or service. In the 1990s, businesses were still learning how things worked, and the Internet was still relatively new. Bezos viewed the setback as an essential milestone and the first of many vital trials that would open up Amazon to outside vendors. The business realized that the network effect of eBay bound small merchants on the Web, so the zShops platform, which had developed from Auctions, was doomed to failure. Bezos was, in fact, the most well-known consumer of these auction ventures. Once, for $40,000, he bought an entire Ice Age cave bear skeleton and put it on display in the foyer of Amazon's brand-new headquarters at the Pacific Medical Center building along with a notice that said, "PLEASE DON'T FEED THE BEAR."

In October 2002, Amazon expanded its product range to include clothes sales, having partnered with hundreds of merchants such as Nordstrom, The Gap, and Land's End. Additionally, they established an Amazon Services subsidiary that lets users purchase products from websites that share the same brand, such as Toys R Us and Borders. Amazon introduced A9, a paid search engine targeted at e-commerce websites, in 2003. They launched an online sports goods store with over 3,000 brands at the same time. Because of Amazon's quick growth, Bezos tested out new service offerings and product lines. Some, like Amazon's effort to sell jewels, were a failure. Some, however, such as Amazon Prime, which, for an annual charge of $79, provided free two-day shipping within the United States, proved to be a huge hit. Because of Prime's popularity, Amazon launched in Italy, France, Germany, the UK, Canada, and Japan in the following ten years. Amazon Prime's service not only guaranteed client loyalty but also set Amazon apart from its rivals.

When Amazon released the Amazon Kindle line of e-readers in 2007, they made yet another technological advance. Going back to the original page where the firm was founded, Bezos aimed to change how consumers obtained books, and the Kindle series was groundbreaking in its intent. Many people believe that the Kindle was the main factor in the internationalization of the e-book business. Before Apple threatened the Kindle's dominance with the release of the iPad in 2010, this portable reading gadget assisted Amazon in securing 95% of the US book market. Bezos responded by lowering the selling price of the Kindle and including new features.

2011 saw Amazon launch the Kindle Fire, a tablet computer designed to take direct aim at Apple's iPad to give the latter company a run for its money. Although Amazon's net income growth is still erratic, it is impressive that the company's sales revenue increased by 122.56% from $48.08 billion in 2011 to $107.01 billion in 2015. For instance, in 2014, Amazon's negative net income growth decreased by $241 million. Nonetheless, Amazon's net income increased positively in 2015, hitting $596 million. However, the net income rise seems insignificant compared to the quickly increasing sales revenue. Bezos intends to first build brand awareness by forgoing revenues. "It would be a bad decision to be profitable [now]," Jeff stated to PC Week in 1998. Jeff told Entrepreneur.com, "If you believe in investing in the future, this is a critical formative time." Most of Amazon's earnings have been allocated to marketing and promotion by Bezos, who wants to dominate the industry. The price of an Amazon share in 1997 was $18.00, while in 2016, it was $549.42.

A comprehensive range of worldwide computing, storage, database, analytics, application, and deployment services are offered by Amazon Web Services, which Jeff Bezos founded in 2006. Thanks to a number of subsidiaries, including a2z, A9.com, Amazon Web Services, Alexa Internet, Audible.com, comiXology, Digital Photography Review, Goodreads, Internet Movie Database, Junglee.com, Twitch, and Zappos, they can now use Amazon's online infrastructure technology for business clients. The website introduced Amazon Studios in 2012, a Kickstarter-like crowdsourcing platform dedicated solely to producing feature films and TV series.

Bezos aimed to become one of the most well-known individuals on the Internet, revolutionize the book trade, and pioneer e-commerce, to name a few. Jeff had always had lofty goals that seemed unattainable, but Amazon's success allowed him to fulfill his enormous dreams fully. His mother has a transcript of a talk Bezos gave back in school, in which he described his plan to build a fleet of habitable orbiting space stations and turn the planet into one enormous nature reserve. He never for once gave up on this goal.

Blue Origin is an aerospace firm that Bezos started in 2004 with the ultimate objective of creating "an enduring human presence in outer space." The organization's mission is to research new technologies for spaceflight. The business operates a private rocket launch site in West Texas and a 26-acre research complex south of Seattle. November 24, 2015: When Blue Origin tested its New Shepard spacecraft, they made news when they launched a rocket into suborbital space and safely landed it on a landing site after takeoff.

The multi-passenger rocket-powered New Shepard aims to provide affordable suborbital space travel. Since no other space business has accomplished a similar achievement, the rocket landing has been dubbed "historic." If this mission is successful, spaceflight costs will drop significantly, and there will be a greater chance for the general population to participate in space travel.

A short while later, SpaceX CEO Elon Musk and Jeff Bezos got into a heated Twitter dispute about their rockets.

Bezos made headlines on August 5, 2013, when he paid $250 million in cash to buy The Washington Post as a whole. Donald E. Graham, chairman and CEO of the corporation, states, "The Post could have survived under the company's ownership, but we wanted to do more than survive." While it increases our chances of success, I'm not arguing that this ensures it. Bezos said his goal was to bring The Washington Post's attention back to the people, not to change the publication's core principles. Bezos is renowned for having a dual nature that causes him to appear friendly but be a tough CEO who commands his staff to respect and fear him. Being very clever and motivated, he anticipates that everyone around him will act the same way. It's alleged that his harsh outbursts, such as "Why are you wasting my life?" and "Are you lazy or just incompetent?" have caused dread and anxiety among the ranks of the Amazon crew.

Jeff Bezos appears to easily manage the firm while personally reviewing customer reviews. Each of them reveals something about our processes; therefore, we investigate them all. It's an audit that our clients perform for us. As senior vice president Jeff Wilke of Amazon clarifies, we value them as valuable information sources. When there is a genuine problem, the accountable personnel may face severe repercussions. Amazon has an established mechanism that assigns a severity rating to internal emergencies.

Bezos always works harder, moves more quickly, and seeks big and small discoveries. Not only is Amazon the everything shop, but it's also the everything corporation, contributing to its fantastic image. There is a bright future ahead of Amazon. Although they still haven't succeeded in offering Prime members same-day or even next-day delivery, Amazon Fresh is still planning to grow outside of Seattle, Los Angeles, and San Francisco. Jeff Bezos anticipates Amazon to rapidly expand into as many nations as feasible. Additionally, they want their consumers to be able to produce their goods utilizing 3D printing technology, doing away with the need to purchase them from manufacturers.

It's unclear if Jeff Bezos's vivid imagination and crazy ideas stem from his early fascination with science fiction or if they are just his personality characteristics. Bezos is renowned for his ability to think creatively and for breaking or reshaping conventions. Bezos consistently breaks the mold, from reinventing how we purchase and read books to starting a people-focused private spaceflight firm to introducing a proposal for package delivery using drones. He thinks creativity is sparked by deviating from the norm and making these bold choices. It's the one thing all great leaders appear to have in common. Unless Jeff Bezos chooses to stop or no one is there to stop him, he will only grow larger and his ideas more outrageous.

Jeff and MacKenzie Bezos' family has four children: three sons and a Chinese-adopted girl. Jeff Bezos and his wife, MacKenzie, announced the ending of their 25-year marriage on January 09, 2019. In addition to giving up her stake in the Washington Post and Blue Origin, MacKenzie relinquished her ex-husband Jeff 75% of their formerly joint Amazon shares.

The life narrative of Jeff Bezos demonstrates that his perseverance, hard work, and unique leadership traits were the main factors in all of his achievements.

The Secrets of Jeff Bezos' Success

Bezos had a vision of an internet store when he quit his secure position in finance. He picked books since they were the most common commodity he could give the most variety. He selected that route because books were so firmly embedded in culture.

With the internet's rapid development at the time, Bezos recognized that he had a limited window of opportunity to build a large corporation. When they first started, they programmed a bell to ring whenever an order was received. It was usually a family member. But the first time they received an order from a stranger, it marked the start of something extraordinary.

The bell rang so frequently within the first 30 days that they had to turn it off. Amazon has expanded since then. Today, it is a massive multi-trillion-dollar corporation ingrained in the everyday lives of hundreds of millions of people who rely on it.

So, how did Jeff Bezos get so powerful? I'll share some of his success secrets with you here.

- **Tip 1: Obsess with Your Customers**

Many businesspeople overlook this basic reality. This transcends the hypothesis that the consumer is always right. To succeed, you must be completely obsessed with your consumers. So, how do you go about achieving this?

According to Bezos, everything they do is about the consumers and what will benefit them the most. Unfortunately, this does not always pay off right away. You waste energy and money to make your consumers happy when you obsess over them.

You do this not simply because finding new consumers is more expensive than selling to existing ones. You do it because it is the right thing you ought to do. That is not just Bezos' perspective; the world's finest businesses share it too.

This implies that each choice must be made with the best interests of the consumers in mind.

- ## Tip 2: Invent and Solve Problems

According to Bezos, you should not wait for the consumer to tell you how to fix an issue. Instead, you must create to answer their difficulties. And it must be done without prodding from the consumer. To build a long-lasting customer-centric firm, you must be inventive.

This does not have to be ground-breaking. It simply implies that you must tackle difficulties in novel ways. What are your thoughts on this? Amazon, for example, has had several issues with duplicate orders, delivery to incorrect locations, and so on.

Bezos claims that users were purchasing negative products early on and receiving payment as credit to their credit cards. Fortunately, the issue was immediately resolved. But the idea is that you must recognize issues and find solutions when they exist.

Amazon began labelling previously ordered products with a duplicate order label to assist customers in avoiding placing a duplicate order. They've also improved operations and included photographs of delivery to combat fraud and wrong-address deliveries.

Tip 3: Think Long Term

In business, it's simple to see why most individuals think in the short term. After all, the majority of enterprises are in survival mode. However, one significant secret to Amazon's success has been to plan considerably further forward. Bezos always plans forward 5 to 7 years.

He claims that such activities do not immediately generate a profit for the corporation. They do, however, immediately bring value to the buyer. However, most of the company's investments do not produce fruit for a long period.

Consider it the next time you decide to launch an initiative, produce a product, or achieve anything noteworthy. When you consider the long term, you shift your emphasis away from competitors and towards your customers.

- **Tip 4: Always Try New Things**

When Bezos says it's always day one, he implies they're flexible in the specifics but firm in their goal. They aren't hesitant to attempt new things, even if things are going well, hoping to improve them.

This follows from being overly focused on the consumer. When you embrace this strategy, you're constantly eager to try new things to improve the customer experience. That is why it is (and will always be) day one at Amazon.

When you consider this notion, it implies that you do not adopt a stodgy attitude to business. Most firms have a strict strategy and do not encourage thinking beyond the box. But not at Amazon, where everything is always on Day One.

It is prioritized if anything will help the client solve an issue or advance another activity.

Without question, Bezos is a very disciplined man. If you lack discipline, that's a good place to start on your path to leadership success. Discipline necessitates the integration of many aspects of your life, such as objectives, routines, and time management. However, without it, success is impossible.

But, before making a critical choice in company or life, ask yourself, "Would these great leaders I've learned about do this?" I know it sounds basic and common. However, given what you know about outstanding leaders and entrepreneurs, the answer to this question may point you in the right direction.

Elon Musk

On June 28, 1971, Elon Musk was given birth to in Pretoria, South Africa. He was the eldest of three siblings. Errol Musk, a South African-born British engineer, is his father, and Maye Musk, a Canadian-English and dietetics specialist, is his mother. Musk grew up in South Africa, and at the age of nine, he received his first personal computer, the Commodore VIC-20. Elon became instantly interested in programming and began to teach himself. At age 12, he made $500 by selling his computer game Blastar (a shooter akin to Space Invaders).

After graduating from a secondary school in Pretoria, he left his home and went to the United States without the backing of his parents. He did not, however, enter the United States straight away.

Elon Musk travelled to Canada in 1989 to live with his mother's family. Elon travelled to Montreal after obtaining Canadian citizenship. He began by working in low-wage jobs and was on the verge of poverty for over a year. He enrolled at Queens University in Kingston, Ontario, at age 19. He met his future wife, Justine Musk, in 2000, and she gave birth to their five kids, Damian, Gryphon, Xavier, Saxon, and Kai. He divorced Justine after eight years and married for the second time in 2010 to a British actress named Talulah Riley, with whom he has been living for four years. In 2014, he divorced.

Elon Musk studied in Ontario for two years before realizing his goal and relocating to the United States in 1992. After winning a scholarship from The University of Pennsylvania, he emigrated to the United States. The following year, he received his Bachelor of Science in Physics. However, he continued his studies for an additional year at the Wharton School of the University of Pennsylvania. He graduated with a Bachelor of Science in Economics as well.

Musk realized that society needed to extend its awareness to learn to ask the proper questions, and he had identified his question: what items would substantially influence mankind's fate in the future? Elon Musk chose the Internet, the shift to renewable energy sources, and space colonization as his top three priorities. He wanted to attempt to help all three of them. He required money to do so.

Elon Musk made the second and most crucial choice in the summer of 1995. After graduating from the University of Pennsylvania, he attended graduate school at Stanford University to study applied physics and materials science. However, after only two days, he dropped out of graduate school and co-founded Zip2 with his brother, Kimbal Musk. He worked from early in the morning till late in the evening. He lived in the same warehouse where he rented the office, and he had to shower at the locker rooms of a nearby stadium.

In exchange, he saved money and kept the firm viable throughout its most challenging first two years.

The Internet was undergoing significant growth and development then, but no one had ever made a substantial fortune from it. Musk's firm was among the first to do so: he established a platform through which newspapers, including reputable ones like the New York Times, could give their consumers extra commercial services.

AltaVista, the largest search engine at the time (later acquired by Compaq), paid $307 million in cash and $34 million in securities to buy Zip2 in 1999. This transaction broke the record for selling a corporation for cash. Musk paid $20 million to extensively refurbish a 1,800-square-foot apartment. He also purchased a McLaren F1, which he crashed in 2000, and a 12-seat Dassault 900 private plane.

Musk began working on electronic payment systems, which were gaining popularity in 1999. His latest venture was the X.com startup. In March 2000, X.com merged with a competitor, Confinity, which Peter Thiel and Max Levchin ran. Confinity created the first digital wallet by developing software that allowed users of PalmPilots and other PDAs to keep encrypted information on their devices. Following the transaction, X.com was renamed PayPal, and Elon Musk was appointed chairman and CEO of PayPal.

There were arguments about strategy and management among the new teams, but they had little impact on the company's dynamics or growth. Musk worked on new business models and ran a successful viral marketing campaign, resulting in a significant consumer rise.

PayPal was bought for $1.5 billion by eBay in 2002. Elon Musk earned $180 million from PayPal for his stake, allowing him to pursue his other interests, which include space engineering and alternative energy sources. Elon ceased investing in the Internet company at that point.

Marc Tarpenning and Martin Eberhard, these two engineers, founded Tesla Motors in 2003. From the start, the firm positioned itself as the first serial manufacturer of electric cars, and its founders hoped to relieve consumers of their need for oil. Musk was a strong supporter of such ambitions.

Elon Musk joined the project in 2004, leading an investment round in the firm with a $70 million personal commitment. He was elected chairman of the board of directors but did not take over the operational administration of the firm at first. Musk was involved in the design of Tesla's first electric vehicle, a Tesla Roadster sports car based on the British Lotus Elise. He insisted on employing carbon fiber composite materials in the hull to save weight and developing the battery module and other design aspects like the headlamps. By 2006, the project had made headlines, and Musk was awarded the Global Green 2006 product design award for the Tesla Roadster. Tesla Motors continued to develop, and the pool of investors now includes Google co-founders Larry Page and Sergey Brin, with a total investment of more than $100 million.

However, as the Tesla Roadster was poised to enter production in 2007, Musk's terrible luck began. Due to several management problems, the actual selling price of the electric car was nearly twice as high as the previously assumed price of $92,000. Furthermore, Martin Eberhard made a strategic error: his Tesla Roadster gearbox plan proved inadequate, forcing the car's introduction to be delayed for more than a year.

During this moment, Elon demonstrated exceptional critical management abilities by firing everyone impeding the project's progress, including Eberhard and other crucial personnel. He took over the corporation after the cleaning. After being replaced by Michael Marks, an interim CEO, Eberhard filed an appeal with the court. Nonetheless, the situation was resolved amicably and effectively, with no information of the disagreement leaking to the public. Ze'ev Drori was named CEO and President of Tesla Motors in December 2007. Elon Musk, who succeeded Ze'ev Drori, was a far superior CEO. Drori was appointed Vice Chairman before leaving the firm in December 2008.

On the cusp of a disaster, Elon Musk aggressively slashed costs: he decreased workers, requested cheaper pricing from suppliers, shuttered certain offices, and so on. As a result, the Tesla Roadster debuted in 2008 with a modest price rise (less than $20,000).

In the late spring of 2008, Elon filed for divorce from his wife, Justine, for reasons he did not wish to discuss publicly. To salvage Tesla Motors, Musk secured more money for Dell's $120 million buyout of Everdream, a software development business in which Elon Musk was the primary stakeholder. He invested his final $20 million in Tesla Motors, preventing the firm from going bankrupt. Musk even personally guaranteed refunds to consumers in the event of a company collapse.

Things moved quickly, which was incredibly amazing given the stagnant traditional auto sector. Daimler, a German global automobile manufacturer, provided a key $50 million investment in Tesla Motors, which helped salvage the firm. Soon after, the US Department of Energy authorized Tesla Motors to be included in a pool of innovative transportation enterprises and to receive a favorable interest-bearing loan. Later, several sceptics chastised the government for supporting Tesla Motors, whose product was aimed solely towards rich consumers.

Tesla Motors launched its initial public offering (IPO) on June 29, 2010. It was the second vehicle manufacturer (after Ford) to go public in the United States. Despite being unsuccessful for ten years, Tesla Motors was listed on NASDAQ for $17 a share, attracting over $225 million in investment. It was, without a doubt, the finest time to enter the IPO market. The oil slick caused by British Petroleum's error covered a large portion of the Gulf of Mexico and was still growing, thus bringing up the question of transitioning to other fuels, which seemed more than sensible. One share of Tesla Motors, Inc. stock cost $220.99 on February 5, 2015, and the company's entire market cap was $27.44 billion. Tesla Motors, Inc. (TSLA) is 30% owned by Elon Musk.

The Tesla Model S, a luxury vehicle with a battery that provides 265 miles (426 km) of range in the EPA 5-cycle test, became the key cause for Tesla's financial success. Model S manufacturing began in June 2012, with prices beginning at $69,900. Consumer Reports gave it 99 out of 100 points, while the National Highway Safety Administration gave it the highest safety grade, 5.4 out of 5 points.

Musk claimed unequivocally during the Model S unveiling that in twenty years, more than half of all vehicles made would be electric. He was even willing to wager on it, as were many others. Even the most optimistic observers believe Musk's projection will not be realized. That, however, does not frighten Tesla's CEO: he alters reality by exaggerating it.

Elon Musk feels the world has become overly reliant on oil. This reliance causes climate change and ongoing geopolitical problems. It can make a difference by avoiding internal combustion engines and favoring electric motors. As a result, Musk's stake in Tesla Motors is substantial.

Musk maintained public interest in the firm by engaging in a media debate with The New York Times writer John M. Broder about one of the Model S test rides. It's worth noting that these publicity stunts yielded results. In the first six months of 2013, 10,500 Model S were sold.

The Tesla Motors team introduced the Model S 85D and P85D on October 9, 2014. This is the first dual-motor electric vehicle. The Model S P85D features a 691-horsepower motor and a 'crazy mode' acceleration of 3.2 seconds from 0-60 mph (0-97 kmh). Furthermore, the vehicle may be outfitted with a novel autopilot system, which includes a forward-facing camera, radar, and 360-degree ultrasonic sensors that actively monitor the surrounding route. With the autopilot system engaged, the Model S can autonomously change lanes, detect and avoid pedestrians and crashes, and even read speed limit signs and appropriately alter the vehicle's speed.

Furthermore, the new Model S has a larger battery capacity. The starting price is $79,900. Visually, the car will resemble its predecessor, the Model S 60. Consumer Reports named the Tesla Model S the best automobile in the world for the second year in February 2014.

Elon Musk intends to build a network of Supercharger stations across the United States, Europe, and Asia. There are 613 Supercharger stations and 3,628 Superchargers globally as of 2016.

Musk introduced the new Tesla Semi Truck and Roadster in November 2017. Tesla Motors began manufacturing semi-trucks in 2019. The vehicle has a range of 500 miles (804 km) and a battery capacity of 1 million miles (1,60 million kilometers).

Musk unveiled the long-awaited Tesla Model Y to the world in March 2019. Standard Range, Long Range, Long Range with Dual Motor All-Wheel Drive, and Performance powertrains will be offered for the small crossover.

Tesla Motors launched the Powerwall, a wall-mounted, rechargeable lithium-ion battery with liquid temperature management, as part of the Tesla Energy initiative in 2015. There are two models: one with 10 kWh and a price tag of $3,500, suitable for backup applications, and another with 7 kWh and a price tag of $3,000, suitable for daily cycle applications. Arrays of Powerwall batteries can be used to enhance total storage capacity. Every battery comes with a 10-year manufacturer's guarantee.

Tesla Motors offers a solution called Powerpack for highly demanding energy customers. It is appropriate for usage in offices, industrial buildings, and utilities.

After selling his 11% stake in PayPal, he invested $10 million in 2003.

Before being bought by Tesla, SolarCity supplied solar power solutions for homes, companies, and governments. The firm provided many programmes for homes, including the "MyPower" financing programme, solar leasing, and solar power purchase agreement (PPA).

In May 2008, the business developed solar-powered electric systems to power the offices and servers of British Motors and eBay.

Elon Musk then considered establishing a space exploration technology firm (SpaceX) at the turn of the century. He was motivated by the lofty goal of lowering space transportation costs so that humanity may colonize Mars. SpaceX was created in 2002 and is based in Hawthorne, California, in the United States.

Elon Musk was enthralled by the prospect of colonizing Mars and founded Mars Oasis. The project's purpose was to build automated greenhouses that might serve as the foundation for a self-sustaining ecosystem in the future. The biggest issue was the exorbitant expense of transporting greenhouses to Mars. Musk also attempted to order launch vehicles from the Russian Federation and spoke with Russian authorities about it, but he chose not to do so. Musk later developed the concept of building reusable launch rockets and spacecraft.

Elon Musk committed more than $100 million to SpaceX in March 2006. Prices for launch vehicles varied from $15 million in Russia to $65 million in the United States, which appeared excessive to the entrepreneur. He calculated that the cost of all the parts needed to build a launch vehicle was just 2% of the price in the United States. This information infuriated Musk. He recognized the basis of the problem in the space industry's bureaucratization, huge businesses' weak competitiveness, and their lobbying attempts to keep new players out.

Musk was promised that the expenses of developing and launching vehicles and spaceships could be cut by a factor of 10. First, he had to rethink the purpose of spaceflights. SpaceX's primary aim is not to bring humans and goods into space but to colonize distant worlds such as Mars, and Musk intends to accomplish this efficiently. Founders Fund, which belongs to Elon Musk's old PayPal associates Peter Thiel and Dave McClure, was one of the first investors to financially back him in August 2008. Steve Jurvetson organized an unknown investment round for DFJ Venture in June 2009, including Founders Fund, which completed at least $15 million of the projected $60 million. SpaceX received $50.2 million in funding from DFJ Venture and Founders Fund in November 2010. Despite this, Elon Musk controls 66% of SpaceX after all the funding rounds.

In 2002, SpaceX began developing the Falcon 1 launch system. It took four years and hundreds of millions of dollars in private financing to design. Companies such as DARPA, NASA, ORS, Celestis, ATSB, SpaceDev, Orbcomm, NSPO, and Astrium were interested in SpaceX and conducted many test flights of the Falcon 1 rocket from 2006 to 2015.

The first three flying attempts failed in 2006-2008. After its fourth flying attempt, Falcon 1 ultimately entered orbit on September 28, 2008. SpaceX would not have been if the fourth launch also failed. NASA was so impressed with these accomplishments that it secured a $1.6 billion contract to transport American astronauts to and from Earth orbit. NASA intends to carry out 12 delivery missions utilizing SpaceX's robotic Dragon spacecraft and Falcon 9 rocket.

As of October 2012, SpaceX had built numerous rocket engines, including Kestrel, Merlin 1, Draco, and Super Draco, without government assistance. The last was created for the Falcon launch vehicle family, which includes the Falcon 1, Falcon 9, Falcon Heavy, and Dragon spacecraft.

Elon Musk, on the other hand, does not want to hurry into an IPO this time. According to Elon Musk, all of SpaceX's accomplishments serve as a backdrop for his ultimate goal: a Mars trip. SpaceX is designing the Mars Colonial Transporter. Musk's engineers are also working on novel rocket engines (the Grasshopper and Falcon 9 rockets) and the Red Dragon spacecraft, which uses Falcon Heavy rockets (a modified version of the Dragon capsule) to take humans from Earth to Mars. He said, "I would like to die on Mars, just not on impact."

Musk introduced The Digging Company in January 2017, a company committed to digging and creating tunnels for automobiles to minimize city street gridlock. Musk began with a test tunnel at SpaceX's Los Angeles headquarters. He posted the first shot of the tunnel on his Instagram account in October 2017. The test tunnel was scheduled to be 2 miles (3.31 km) long, and Musk expected to complete it in four months.

According to reports, Elon Musk's Boring Company is working on a hyperloop project named "X-Tunnel." The idea is still in its early phases, but Musk has stated that he aims to create a hyperloop tube connecting Los Angeles and San Francisco.

In April 2022, Elon Musk took over the social media business Twitter, Inc. By April, he had become the company's top stakeholder, with a 9.1 per cent ownership position, after beginning to acquire shares in January 2022. Musk said that he intended to fight spambot accounts that pose as real people by using false profiles, add new features to the platform, make its algorithms open-source so that anyone interested in studying them could do so, and support free speech on Twitter by enabling anyone to post anything they want without restriction. Following Elon Musk's takeover of the firm in October 2022, Twitter was rebranded X on July 23, 2023.

Elon Musk stated in one of his interviews that he enjoys reading novels and biographies of notable individuals, such as "Benjamin

Franklin: An American Life" by Walter Isaacson, "Tesla: Inventor of the Electrical Age" by B. Carlson, "Structures: Or Why Things Don't Fall Down" by J.E. Gordon, and others.

He also enjoys Dale Carnegie's writings and a wide range of engineering, design, business, and physics literature. Douglas Adams' "The Hitchhiker's Guide to the Galaxy" is Elon's favorite book.

Elon Musk is a twenty-first-century businessman who brings extraordinary ideas to reality. Elon Musk's life biography demonstrates that his success was due to his dedication, hard work, and unwavering trust in his initiatives. I hope you liked learning about Elon Musk's life and the success of Tesla Motors and SpaceX.

The Secrets of Elon Musk's Success

- **Tip 1: Have Enthusiasm**

Elon has often stated that he doesn't care about money and that all of his fortune is derived from Tesla shares; therefore, if Tesla fails, so does he. He is not in this company to generate money; rather, he is there because he is a fervent supporter of space travel and renewable energy, and he wants to realize his dreams of living on Mars and doing away with fossil fuels. It's okay if your enthusiasm for Mars isn't as strong as Elon's. Everyone has various interests and passions. You must follow your passions and engage in occupations and pastimes that you genuinely like. Elon Musk's success is driven by his passion.

- ## Tip 2: Strive for Excellence

The term "ambitious" sums up Elon Musk better than any other. Whatever your opinion of his concepts, it's impossible to deny that they're ambitious—literally, in SpaceX's case. The lesson here is to not restrict oneself. As noted by the great thinker Norman Vincent Peale, if you aim for the moon, you will still land among the stars, even if you miss it. Setting high standards for yourself ensures that you will still achieve something amazing, even if you fall short of your objectives. SpaceX will probably land on Mars eventually, but even if it doesn't, consider all the incredible achievements the firm has already made in developing cutting-edge rockets. Set your sights higher than the outcome you'll be content with.

- ## Tip 3: Keep Learning

This is one piece of advice that works for everyone. You must never give up attempting to expand your knowledge of the world and yourself. Elon has always been vocal about this, frequently sharing reading lists of books that he believes would transform your life and his. He's also discussed the idea that you don't need to attend college or a school to continue learning. Official education is undoubtedly important, but you can learn just as much by reading interesting books, watching documentaries you would not have otherwise, and even listening to others with different opinions. Foster and feed your never-ending need for knowledge.

- **Tip 4: Allow Space for Growth**

Compared to a "fixed mindset," Musk is arguably the most well-known businessman with a "growth mindset." This implies having faith in your ability to acquire new abilities and hone your current ones. It permits creativity, advancement, and adaptability if a plan ought to be modified after it fails. These are chances for you to advance your projects and yourself, which is the essence of adopting a development mindset. Allow yourself to be open to new chances, even if they don't come your way.

- **Tip 5: Have No Fear of Failure**

It's normal to be terrified of making mistakes and losing your face. But you have to accept failure if you want to succeed in life at some point. Consider a failure as a teaching opportunity instead of an irreversible catastrophe. With every setback, you gain increasingly useful skills that will propel you forward. It's true what they say: "Try again if you don't succeed the first time." Despite the company's many well-publicized setbacks over the years, SpaceX has not folded altogether. No, it indicates that Musk and his several highly skilled scientists and engineers will not give up.

- **Tip 6: Take Risks**

You will be unstoppable and able to take significant risks to achieve your goals after you have conquered your fear of failing. Over the years, Musk has often stated that becoming the man he is now results from his willingness to take calculated risks. According to him, taking such types of risks becomes more difficult as a company expands, and more individuals are held accountable if something goes wrong, so take early and bold risks. Take up a hobby or activity you've always wanted to try, start the small business you believe has the potential to succeed, or start writing the novel you've always wanted to!

As we've seen, several elements, such as Elon Musk's creative thinking, daring nature, and dedication to social impact, contributed to his success.

This chapter has examined the lives, success stories, and trade secrets of extremely successful people in business, leadership, and general success. As you can see, a highly effective leader needs certain abilities, traits, and a dedication to lifelong learning. By putting these extremely successful leaders' secrets into practice, you may realize your leadership potential, propel corporate success, and have a big effect on the globe. It's important to remember to create a clear vision, promote responsibility and trust, accept flexibility, stimulate creativity, cultivate strong bonds, set a good example, promote teamwork, enhance emotional intelligence, assign tasks skillfully, and prioritize self-care. Accept these tips, and you'll open the door to a fruitful and satisfying career as a leader.

Conclusion

Creating a Lasting Legacy

"Legacy is not leaving something for people. It's leaving something in people." – Peter Strople

When leaders fail, their reputation and legacy suffer. It is difficult to leave a lasting legacy. Dedication, time, and work are required for your legacy. There will always be instances when you must sacrifice your vision or principles to accomplish your goals. This can be challenging, but it is frequently required.

A leader's legacy is their permanent imprint on their team, company, and the larger community. It is the effect that shapes and influences others even after the leader has passed away. A legacy is more than a person's personal accomplishments or financial success; it is about the good and long-term transformation a leader delivers to the lives of the people they lead.

Leaving a leadership legacy is more than a nice-to-have; it is a necessary component of good leadership. A leader's influence lasts well beyond their tenure, impacting the team and organization's

189

culture, values, and performance. A great legacy inspires and encourages team members, instilling purpose and devotion. It also attracts top talent, as individuals gravitate toward firms with a reputation for strong and influential leadership.

To conclude this fascinating book, I will share some crucial considerations for creating and leaving a wonderful, enduring legacy.

Make Your Vision Clear

A successful leadership legacy is built on a compelling vision. Take the time to develop your team's and organization's vision, then express it clearly and consistently. A well-defined vision creates a feeling of purpose and direction, directing decision-making and encouraging people to work together toward a common objective.

Develop a Positive Culture

Culture has a huge impact on a leader's legacy. Create an atmosphere that encourages cooperation, respect, and creativity. Encourage open communication, give your team members influence, and foster a sense of belonging and inclusion. A positive culture improves team morale and performance and has a long-term influence on the corporate culture.

Encourage Mentorship and Development

Investing in the growth and development of your team members is an important part of leaving a legacy. Mentor and coach your team members actively, assisting them in reaching their full potential. Make learning and development opportunities available and promote ongoing progress. By developing the next generation of leaders, you generate a ripple effect that lasts well beyond your tenure.

Lead with Integrity and Ethics

A successful leadership legacy is built on ethical leadership. In your actions and decisions, show integrity, honesty, and openness. Maintain high ethical standards for yourself and others. Setting the appropriate example and cultivating an environment of ethics and integrity has a long-term influence on your team's individual and collective conduct.

Create High-Performance Teams

Developing high-performing teams is an important part of leaving a leadership legacy. Invest in team growth by concentrating on trust, cooperation, and maximizing individual capabilities. Create a culture of constant learning and progress by encouraging a growth mentality. By cultivating high-performing teams, you not only accomplish extraordinary outcomes but also leave a lasting impression on people and the team as a whole.

Empower Others to Lead

A successful leadership legacy is about enabling others to lead, not simply your successes. Provide possibilities for growth, leadership development, autonomy, and decision-making. Fostering a leadership culture and inspiring others has a long-term influence beyond your career.

Accept Diversity and Inclusion

Embracing diversity and inclusion is critical for establishing a leadership legacy in today's varied and globalized society. Make your workplace an inclusive and equal where everyone feels appreciated and respected. Diversity in ideas, views, and experiences should be encouraged, as diverse teams are more innovative and productive. You leave a legacy of equality and opportunity by advocating diversity and inclusion.

Encourage an Innovative Culture

In today's fast-paced corporate world, innovation is a critical driver of success. Encourage exploration, inventiveness, and risk-taking. Provide resources and assistance for innovation projects and recognize and reward creative ideas and accomplishments. Promoting an innovative culture has a long-term influence on an organization's capacity to adapt and survive in a quickly changing world.

Leaving a leadership legacy is a continuous process, not a one-time event. It necessitates ongoing self-reflection, learning, and development. You can make a lasting impression on your team and company by defining your vision, developing a good culture, supporting mentoring and growth, leading with ethics and integrity, and embracing practical tactics. Remember that it is not just about what you achieve as a leader but also about the good and transformative change you bring to the lives of others around you.

www.ingramcontent.com/pod-product-compliance
Lightning Source LLC
Chambersburg PA
CBHW070859290526
45795CB00001B/180